HERE I AM
THE WRITING AND ART OF EMILIA ALMADA

Robert Almada

Author's Tranquility Press
Marietta, Georgia

Copyright © 2021 by Robert Almada.

All rights reserved. No part of this publication may be reproduced, distributed or transmitted in any form or by any means, including photocopying, recording, or other electronic or mechanical methods, without the prior written permission of the publisher, except in the case of brief quotations embodied in critical reviews and certain other noncommercial uses permitted by copyright law. For permission requests, write to the publisher, addressed "Attention: Permissions Coordinator," at the address below.

Robert Almada/Author's Tranquility Press
2706 Station Club Drive SW
Marietta, GA 30060
www.authorstranquilitypress.com

Publisher's Note: This is a work of fiction. Names, characters, places, and incidents are a product of the author's imagination. Locales and public names are sometimes used for atmospheric purposes. Any resemblance to actual people, living or dead, or to businesses, companies, events, institutions, or locales is completely coincidental.

Ordering Information:
Quantity sales. Special discounts are available on quantity purchases by corporations, associations, and others. For details, contact the "Special Sales Department" at the address above.

Here I Am/Robert Almada
Hardcover: ISBN: 978-1-956480-88-7
Paperback: ISBN: 978-1-956480-87-0
EBook: ISBN: 978-1-956480-89-4

Dedication

In loving memory of my husband Ignacio Almada

Table of Contents

PART I
SHORT STORIES BY EMILIA ALMADA

HERE I AM	3
ROAMING FRANCE AND SPAIN	4
MY TRIP TO FRANCE IN 1983	4
FROM FRANCE TO SPAIN	11
BACK TO FRANCE	16
MY ADVENTURES IN SOUTHERN FRANCE	20
OUR TRIP TO MEXICO IN THE YEAR 1979	23
MY LAST TRIP TO MEXICO	26
913 BLUE ISLAND AVENUE	29
END OF A BUSY DAY	32
JANUARY 1989 – OUR MONTH TRIP WEST	33
DREAMS	39
IN LOVING MEMORY OF MY HUSBAND IGNACIO	40
A TRIP TO THE MOUNTAINS	41
GOOD DAY FOR A RUN – LITTLE EMOTION	42
MY THIRD GRADE EXPERIENCE	43
YOUNG EMILIA	44
MY GREATEST CHALLENGE AS A WRITER	47
REGRETS REGRETS	48
REVIEWING LIFE WHILE WAITING AT A LIGHT	49
EMILIA AT THE ART FAIR	50
A LEARNING EXPERIENCE	53
THE VAGABOND (*ITALIAN*)	55
WE MOVED TO NORTHLAKE	56
AFTER GRADUATION FROM HIGH SCHOOL	57
IS THAT ALL THERE IS	60
DREAMS AND FRIENDS	61

PART II
THE ART WORKS OF EMILIA ALMADA

CERAMICS	67
BEST OF SHOW	67
LAMPS	81

PAINTINGS	83
CHALK	93
NEEDLE WORK	94
ACKNOWLEDGEMENTS	100
THE END	101

INTRODUCTION

This book gives the reader a look into the mind of Emilia Almada. In Part I you will find stories, poems and musings based on her personal experiences. They span a lifetime of memories. In Part II you will get a peek at the artistic side of Emilia. The art works were created at different stages of her life as a mother, a wife and a widow.

Emilia was born in Mexico in 1919 and was brought to Chicago when she was 3 years old. Her native language was Spanish but she learned English quickly and grew up being fluent in both languages. As an adult she learned to speak French and Italian. She married Ignacio Almada whom she lovingly referred to as Ig or Nacho. They had 8 children. While raising a family, she maintained a light exercise routine and showed talent in writing, creating drawings made with pencil and dark and colored chalk, paintings that were originals and copies, ceramics that were practical and/or artistic, and needle works which included sewing, crocheting and knitting. She wrote a book, "The Saga of Millie & Ig – The Long Road Home" where she detailed the lives of both her and Ignacio Almada from their respective childhoods to their meeting and starting a family together.

We, her children, decided to take the short stories she had written and much of her art work and put them into this book as a celebration of her 99th birthday. Enjoy!

Edited by Robert Almada

PART I

SHORT STORIES BY EMILIA ALMADA

HERE I AM

Here I am. How did I get here? For many years I've breathed this air that came to me at birth. I have passed through many doors, walked many miles. Some of those miles were easy, some were very difficult. Along my path I have passed some sunny streets and some dark tunnels. Many of the people I have met and walked with were young and vibrant. All along the road I have met and passed people who affected my life, many making that road easier to travel. Then there were those bumps and trumps. All the people I knew when I was young, I see today so changed. Some have even lost their memory either partially or completely. I'm not far behind. Through it all, the years go by and never stop moving on.

Illustration 1: EMILIA - SELF PORTRAIT

ROAMING FRANCE AND SPAIN

MY TRIP TO FRANCE IN 1983

French had been one of the subjects in my curriculum for several years, along with some math and science courses. I had intended to work for my associate degree then continue on to earn a Bachelor's degree. I was getting ready for final exams when I found out that there was going to be a summer class in France. That, I thought, would be great experience for the young people in the class. As for me, I had no intention of going anywhere outside of the USA. At home, I went about my usual tasks when a trip to France was announced on a TV commercial. This trip was being advertised for ten days for the same price the student trip would be, except that the student trip would be for one month and fifteen days. It was unbelievable. I pointed that out to my husband who said that I had to be mistaken. The next day I brought home the brochure on the French trip to prove my point. When my husband saw the brochure, he studied it, and immediately said to me, "you're going!" I mentioned that I was neither interested nor planning on going, but he insisted that I go. I asked him who would cook his meals and wash his clothes and keep him company. He said "Don't worry about me, I'll be just fine." He wanted me to have the experience of studying in France.

Thus it was that I made ready to travel outside of the United States. For this trip one needed a passport, a visa and train passes, as well as money orders needed for the time abroad. We also had to attend several meetings on what to expect in France, as well as what not to do there and how to behave. After all, we did not want to be viewed as the "ugly Americans." After being versed on all the necessities, we were ready to go. All week long I had phone calls from relatives and neighbors wishing me bon voyage.

The day of my departure finally arrived. My husband took me to the airport and stayed till I was ready to board. I boarded the plane that our teacher and a few of the other students were on. The plane was a Sabena 747, which looked like four buildings put together. Could this monstrosity really get up in the air? Well, it did get up in the air and we sailed through the sky in relative comfort. Flight instructions were given in German, French and English. We reached Belgium on Friday at 5 AM, Belgian time. It was midnight back in Chicago. That was when I adjusted my watch and wished that I could lay down somewhere for a long nap. I tried to rest on the flight, but the anticipation of visiting other countries and being away from home for over a month made it difficult.

Most of the students would be arriving a few days later, but some of those who arrived with us left for Paris on a later train that same day. Mr. Smith, our teacher, and three of us stayed to wait for the rest of the students, the three of us being, myself and two young men. We settled in the "Pension," a bed and breakfast, for the evening. I could not get comfortable because, even though it was the last week of May, it was so cold that I felt it to my bones. This was to be my day of celebration, my birthday, but instead I was in total discomfort. Even the blankets did not keep me warm. I slept with my clothes on and hugged myself to be somewhat comfortable. Somehow I survived. The next morning was a Sunday and I decided to find a church for Sunday Mass. I found one nearby where the priest said the Mass in French, which I enjoyed since I understood most everything. After Mass I went for a walk and came upon the town square, where a sort of market place was set up. It reminded me of Maxwell Street in Chicago. From there I went back to the hotel, met with the boys and let them know what I had seen. I also told them about a Spanish restaurant that looked inviting, which seemed to me a good idea to try out for lunch. My companions agreed with me, and off we went. When we got there, we saw that a celebration was going on for a young girl who had just made her confirmation. It looked like it was going to be a great celebration. We however, had come for lunch and before leaving the "Pension" we promised to be back for dinner. On the way back to our rooms, we looked around the area for a while to see if we had missed anything interesting. After looking around, we went back to the "Pension." That afternoon, we decided to play cards before going out for dinner and settling down for the night. That was one way of keeping busy and whiling away the time.

On Monday, (Memorial Day in the USA), it dawned a beautiful day in Brussels. It was warm and sunny, not at all like the past two days. Maybe it was because we would be leaving today. I had spent the morning packing and was ready to go when one of the boys came knocking on my door. We did not even stay for the "petit dejeuner"— (breakfast). Being a short distance away, we walked to the train station with our suitcases and waited for the last three students, who finally appeared with Mr. Smith. He had gone to meet them at the airport. With the arrival of the last students, we made ready to leave Brussels. Before long, it was time to board the train for Paris and we were on our way. We arrived in Paris in the early afternoon and settled in our hotel before meeting the rest of the students. Once we were situated, we realized that we were starving. We began to look for a place to eat, but all the restaurants were closed. We found out that they close at

3:00 in the afternoon and re-open at 7 00 in the evening. What were we to do? In our checking around for a place to have lunch, we found a McDonald's in Paris. I thought McDonald's was only in America. It seemed that the franchise was on a quest to take over the world. However, I was thankful that they were there and open for business when I needed them. We had a quick snack, and then entertained ourselves the best we could until the evening. When the restaurant finally opened, we were in line and ready to order a full meal. After dinner, we all decided to go for a walk along the river Seine before going back to the hotel.

For the few days before leaving for Arcachon, we enjoyed what we could of Paris. We walked to the Louvre Art Museum, saw the Eiffel Tower in the distance, and climbed the "Arc de Triumph." From there, the view of the city was beautiful on all four sides. We also took a long walk along the "Place de la Concorde." It was very exciting for me, being on the other side of the Atlantic and visualizing in my mind all that went on centuries ago. Several of us decided to go for a boat ride on the Seine which was very informative and refreshing. I panicked for a second when I thought about how far I was from my home in the USA. I couldn't walk or drive home, but then calmed down and decided I had to make the best of this opportunity. After all, this was a great chance which I had never expected to come my way. After all these activities and getting acquainted with Paris, we were ready for a good night's rest. The next morning we were ready for more sightseeing after breakfast. This time we got on the Metro and were off to Versailles. It was very impressive to see this wonderful place where so much history was made. We saw the gardens, the palace, and so many paintings of Marie Antoinette, and Napoleon, to mention a few. All in all it was a great day, even though it finished off with a good rain. With so much to see and so much to choose in a short time, we were happy to adhere to our teacher's advice. After supper we returned to our hotel and were ready to rest for a while before going to bed. We had spent four wonderful days in Paris, and made the most we could for the time we had. I promised myself that I would return to Paris to do more visiting and sightseeing. Five days after arriving in Europe, we were on the train for Arcachon, where our French classes would be conducted. There was standing room only on the train for most of us all the way to Bordeaux. I happened to find a seat in one compartment where two ladies were carrying on a conversation, which I listened to and understood some. I also slept some of the way. Arriving at Bordeaux, we had to make our connection for Arcachon. It was a rush to get our tickets, since we only had 15 minutes before the train would be leaving. The entire trip from Paris to Arcachon was a good eight hours. We had not been able to eat while traveling so we were starved by the time we arrived at Arcachon. Before settling in we went to a restaurant to have a much needed dinner. Our place of lodging was an old remodeled house which belonged to a lady named Veronique, a former Triton College teacher. After all this traveling, we were tired and ready for a good night's rest.

Every now and then, I had to tell myself that I was not dreaming; that I actually was here on the other side of the Atlantic Ocean. However, once in Arcachon, we settled down and every morning after breakfast our teacher, Mr. Smith, would bring the class to order. We were to speak only French in and out of our quarters. Along with Mr. Smith, we had a teacher's aide who helped the students when necessary. That aide was a young lady named Rosemary, who was ready to help us and make our learning easy and interesting. She would be living in the same quarters with us.

The day after arriving we settled into our rooms, made our claims as to which drawers we wanted and determined what our days for chores would be. After arriving in Arcachon we all wanted to get acquainted with the post office, so we could send mail to friends and relatives back in the USA. It was also time to get our clothes laundered since we now had a place to do our washing and a place to hang our clothes to dry.

Shopping for food everyday was a necessity and would be done after classes at the local supermarket. This was also a great way to practice the language outside of our quarters. Occasionally, we went into the town to look around as well as to do any other shopping. That was how we figured out where to find what we might need or want.

Our classes were held every weekday morning after breakfast, but on the fifth day Mr. Smith invited the students to his quarters for champagne, cheese, and a light lunch. We enjoyed the afternoon with Mr. Smith, telling stories and making comments, all in French, while finishing the bubbly. Then we all went to a bar called "Bar-Tabac" for more toasting, before going back to our rooms. That was our lesson for Fridays.

All of us were free to visit the town or do anything we cared to do after our class time, but we had to have our homework done by the next class. One of our daily trips was to the post office to send mail, and wait for mail from home, hoping to hear from friends and family in the USA.

There was a beach on the Bay of Biscay, just around the corner, a few steps from our house. We would often go there for a swim or just to watch others swim. Occasionally we would see a boat go sailing by. On one evening, after classes and dinner, we went to the beach where we saw the sun setting while listening to Rosemary play her guitar. It was almost 10:00 PM, but the sun was just starting to set. I enjoyed the evenings and watching the sunset. I imagined sending the sun West to my family in America. It looked so beautiful and unbelievable at that late hour.

There were many shops and sights to get acquainted with in our surroundings. Besides our lessons, we also went on several tours in the most interesting parts of France. This was possible because the school had hired a private bus to take us on several trips. One of our first trips was to the Basque Country on a Friday morning. We boarded the bus and were off on a tour, but our first stop was a nearby town for our morning coffee. I must say that the coffee there was "tres forte," which means very strong.

We passed through a forest on the way to Biarritz where we stopped for a good while to enjoy the view. It reminded me of the California coast around La Jolla. Soon we were back on the bus, but somehow we got lost. We had to turn back and stop to get directions. While waiting we took a walk to admire the area, which was beautiful and led to a place called Romain Pont, (Romain Bridge). In this area we found a fall with rushing water. We continued to walk around, admiring the beautiful scenery. Once back on the bus we were looking for something called La Ruhne, which is the cable tram that climbs up to the summit of the Pyrenees, and we finally found it.

At last we were on the cable tram and on our way to the top of the mountain. That day had been rather cloudy and as we got closer to the top we were enveloped in a very thick cloud, but once we came through the clouds we saw the sun, and also saw that there were people who lived on these mountains. The Basques live there and plant terraces of vegetation and whatever they enjoy and need. They also have herds of animals that feed on the vegetation of the mountains. We walked around on the summit just looking at all the many articles that were for sale and admiring all their handiwork. I had a conversation with a Basque (a Spanish Basco) who explained some of their art as well as their customs. Soon we took the tram back down to the French border, where we boarded our bus and drove to our hotel, a Basque Hotel where we would spend the night. We were served dinner then went back to our rooms with the reminder that we had to be on the road at 8:00 AM. The next morning, after breakfast, (après le petit dejeuner, nous sommes parti pour St.Jean Pied du Port) - we went to visit the town mentioned (St. Jean Pied du Port) - where there was a market place with an abundance of food and goods for sale. We wandered around and looked at all their wares, and some of us did buy a few things. It was all very interesting, but soon we were ready to head towards the river bank for our lunch and to enjoy the surroundings. The viewing of the rushing rivers and cascades coming down the mountain sides and into the river was a sight never to be forgotten. The next morning we started out for Lourdes, but because of the traffic congestion, we had to park a distance away from the entrance. This caused us to hurry, since our time was short, but we decided to take a quick walk through the area. We had gone a short way before we realized that we were lost. We had to retrace our steps and finally reached the area of Lourdes. We got to see the grotto where Bernadette had seen the apparition, but then it was time to get back to the bus or be late for dinner at the next motel. To get to our next destination, we had to cross the Napoleon Bridge. When we got to our hotel, there across the road, we saw rapids rushing down into a cave like opening in the mountain. It was the great fall "La Gav d' Oloron" and a sight to behold. It was so exciting to be so close to that fall that we visited it again while we were there, because it was so amazing! After our dinner, we crossed the bridge into the town, St. Pee-sur Nivelle, where there was a show in progress at a casino. It appeared that different groups of people were enjoying a private show of some sort in their own space. While walking back, we enjoyed the sight of the beautiful mountains against the evening sky. We finished our walk telling stories and singing French and Spanish songs before settling in at our hotel.

The next morning, after breakfast, we were ready for our next excursion. We checked out of the hotel and were on our way to see a church that had been built in the twelfth century. After this excursion, we stopped in a town where we found a horse farm at the foot of a mountain. There we were invited to take a horse ride if we wanted. Our group spent an hour or so enjoying this visit, and then it was time to continue on our trip to Pau, where we got to see the palace of King Henry the 4th of France, the father of King Louis. That was a grand and great palace to see. All the palaces we saw were great and immense, but it is hard to imagine how one could find comfort living in them.

Occasionally we would do single day trips. One of our day trips was to the Perigeaux region. There, we saw some old castles and old churches as well as market places, before going to a special place for dinner. These trips were very enjoyable because we were taken to several different places in France and each place had its particular interests.

After all this traveling, we would go back to our home base. We were usually hungry and tired and slept very well. The next day we would settle into the regular routine of study, shopping for whatever and going to the beach. When we were not on a tour, I occasionally would walk into the town to shop and talk to the local merchants. This was my time for practicing the language and getting acquainted with the town's people. Now and then I would engage a salesperson in a good conversation about his or her business. I enjoyed this very much for the time I was in Arcachon.

It was the middle of June and our classes were now half way done. One of the girls had a birthday during this period. Rosemary made a special cake for her, since this girl had digestive problems. We sang "happy birthday" to her in French, then we were off to the beach where we found the tide was high and the beach was covered with water. Our only choice was to go back home, since the beach was flooded. A few days later it was the Professor's birthday, and again it was time for a celebration. All the students were involved in the preparation of making Mr. Smith's day a happy one. Rosemary made a special cake and prepared dinner for the occasion, and again we sang "happy birthday" in French. All the class, some of our neighbors, and our bus driver, were part of that special day. Every now and then, we would look around our town to see what interesting things might be going on. We found an aquarium in the town and walked through some neighborhoods that looked very exclusive. Also on these walks, we found a movie house. On another occasion, we walked over to see the "pelotte", which is a Basque ball game, sort of like a "Hi Li" type of game, and it was in our area. The ball is hit back and forth with a sort of small basket in hand. The score is rather like tennis, or so at least that is what I understood. On another occasion, we were entertained by a group of musicians who had been in the Andes. The concert was done by four men who had been in South America and learned the music and ways of the Taquila Indians. These men had picked up the style and language of the country they had visited, and were ready to pass it on wherever they could. Some of these entertaining acts were done on the church premises for lack of public halls. At least that seemed the case when I was there. On one of our local shopping excursions, we met our bus driver who invited us to meet his parents and to see his house. It was an old building which they bought and had been remodeling for a few years. It appeared to us that they were succeeding quite well, and we told them so. We met and visited with his family for a while, then had to get back to our place to get dinner ready for the other students. Besides the teaching and excursions, which we participated in during our stay in Arcachon, Mr. Smith and Rosemary had put together a program for the month, which included celebrating the birthdays that came up in that period. One of those celebrations was done at a hotel near the house that we, the students, occupied. The occasion was another birthday of one of the girls, which was to be celebrated at a hotel near the Bay of Biscay. Mr. Smith was well acquainted with Mr. Lovie, the owner of the Hotel St. Christaud. This celebrating was twofold, since beside the birthday, it also was the reuniting of Mr. Lovie and his wife with Mr. Smith and Rosemary. After dinner, we were off to see the parade of boats on the Bay, where we watched them sail away through the evening. It was so enjoyable to be on the beach of the Bay, where we spent many evenings watching the sun go down.

As was mentioned before, the house we were staying in belonged to a former Triton college teacher. She had taught French in Chicago, but now was married and into other ventures with her husband. Her neighbors, the Dagault's, had been hired to take care of the house in Arcachon when the owners traveled. Mr. and Mrs. Dagualt soon became our friends. They invited us to visit the Dunes de Pyla on a weekend. When we got there, I could not believe my eyes. I had never seen such a high mountain of sand, and I never thought I would be able to climb it, but I did. There was a path where one could climb easily and a second path that was more challenging. I chose the rough way. That whole area of a sand mountain was something to see and I was on it. It was exciting and unbelievable finding myself on this vast sand mountain with many others enjoying and romping about. For me, this was a day to remember, but the time came too soon to return to our quarters. That evening Mrs. Dagualt invited me to supper. We had a nice meal after which I visited with her and her husband. We talked about our families and what our interests were. She mentioned that she had lived in California at one time. Finally, after an enjoyable day, it was time to get back to the house and retire.

On the last two days of our month of studies, we finished our assignments, and tests were taken the next morning. Too soon the day came when the classes were over. Most of us then did some quick shopping for souvenirs and a last visit to the Bay. Then it was time to say goodbye to all the people we had come to know and whose company we had enjoyed. Promises were made to remember and to keep in touch with each other. This was one of the occasions when one remembers Shakespeare's "Parting is such sweet sorrow."

FROM FRANCE TO SPAIN

At this point in time, we had two more weeks to use up before leaving for home. It was up to each one of us to spend the two remaining weeks any way we wanted. Most of us wanted to see what we could of the surrounding countries. I and one other student, Licel, decided to visit Spain. Before boarding the train to the border, we sent our heavy luggage to the train station in Paris. Now with our lighter luggage we could travel more at ease. The train took us to the border of France, where we crossed over into Spain, then walked to the train station at the Spanish border. We were ready to board the train to Madrid when it arrived. The train station was empty and around the middle of the day we were informed that the train to Madrid would not be arriving till late in the evening. It was late afternoon and we were getting hungry. There were no concessions or machines to buy food at this station. Knowing we had a long time to wait, we decided to look around the area in hopes of finding a place to get some food. We found a Basque feast that was going on in the town, which included a parade but no food. All this time we had to carry our luggage with us since there were no lockers available. We had enough time to watch the entire parade because our train would be arriving very late. The women and children in the parade were in their native dress. This was entertaining and enjoyable to watch, and it abated our hunger a bit. When the parade was over, we took a walk through the town before going back to the station. The train finally came at just about midnight. Once on the train we fell asleep in our seats with the hope that we would satisfy our hunger in Madrid. We arrived early in the morning, and before leaving the station we made our train reservations for Seville.

The first thing we did in Madrid was check in to our hotel room. El Hotel de Mediodia was our choice, but it was a bad choice since it was next to the expressway. The fumes from the passing cars was terrible, so we closed the window in order to somewhat eliminate those fumes. After a shower and breakfast we wanted to see what was around us. While there we took the Metro to an old neighborhood, where Licel said her family had lived when they were in Spain. There, she found the name and address of a family they had known. She decided to call on them, and they were kind enough to invite us to their home for a short visit. The visit was pleasant, with questions and answers going around. After much conversion we thanked them and left. It was July and very hot in this town. After walking around we had some refreshments and occasionally sat down to rest. The next day we checked out of our hotel and were off to the train station, (-la gare-in French- -in Spanish –La Estacion de Atocha) about 5:00 PM and waited until 9:00 PM for the train to arrive. We boarded the train and were on the way to Seville, where we were hoping to see some real Spanish dancing.

It was Sunday July 3rd about 6:30 AM, when we arrived in Seville. The first thing to do was to get to our hotel room and catch up on our sleep. Our hotel was in the old section of Seville, very close to an old and great Cathedral. The style of houses and buildings was clearly Moorish. In this section of town, the streets are so narrow that it is hard to believe a car could make it through. After looking around, we were hungry and had to quickly find a place to have breakfast. Later that morning we walked through the narrow streets and visited parks, then walked back to the hotel to rest before lunch. After lunch, we decided to go in the opposite direction of where we had gone in the morning. We ran into the river, the Guadalquivir, as well as a beautiful park called the gardens of Maria Luisa. We did not know who Maria Luisa was, but decided to look that up some other time. On the way back to the hotel, we found a sort of tavern or bar, or it seemed like a small theatre, where a concert would be held that evening. We lingered and admired for a while then went back to the hotel for dinner. After all that walking we thought it a good idea to rest before the evening entertainment. In the meantime, I decided to write out some post cards to my husband, just to let him know that I was alright and had not forgotten him. Soon it was time to get ready for that evening's show. Now we knew where the places were that we wanted to spend some time visiting. We walked through the narrow streets again to that place where the Spanish Dance Program would be taking place. There were several of these shows in town, but we chose "Los Gallos" because they were closer to our area. But more important, it was there that the typical authentic Spanish flamenco would be taking place, or so we had heard from different people. We were not disappointed. It really was a beautiful program. The music and the dancing were exhilarating. After the show we were able to talk to the guitarist and the singers for a short while. A Chinese couple sitting next to us was from New York which gave us the opportunity to chat and compare our two great cities. It was about midnight when we got back to our hotel. We had had an enjoyable and interesting evening and were ready to drop into a deep slumber.

The next morning, on the 4th of July, we left the hotel after breakfast and were off to the train station. We made it on time and soon were on our way to Granada, but had to make a connection in a town called Bobadilla. Once we made our connection, we relaxed a bit before arriving at our destination. We arrived at rush hour which was the worst of times. Everyone was in a hurry and tempers were at the very worst, but we had to find a place to stay. The hotel I had chosen was in a very crowded part of town and the room did not have a safety lock, which made it too uncomfortable. There, it also seemed to be heavy with traffic up and down the halls. Licel had put the fee on her credit card, but we felt uncomfortable in this place, so we decided to go somewhere else. We asked for the return of our fee and left. We then went to an area a bit less busy. We found a hotel that felt more comfortable, since it was farther away from the busy part of town. Licel decided that she did not like the town and did not want to stay in Granada. We discussed our options. I had to convince her that we would probably never be back here again and should make the best of our time in Granada. I was trying to weigh my options as well. Should I agree with Licel and leave this town or should I stay on and see what I wanted to see alone before going on? I agreed that this town was a fast moving town, yet I had heard so much about it and the song "Granada" kept spinning in my head. Mostly I wanted to see the Alhambra where the moors had built their palace and citadel back in the 12th and 13th centuries. We decided to wait till morning to check things out.

It was Tuesday morning and we still had decisions to make. We did some shopping after breakfast then went to the train station to check up on the schedules. Licel still wanted to leave, but the line was very long and not moving, so after an hour I told her that I had decided to stay on to see the Alhambra. That had been one of the main reasons for my visit to Granada. She wanted to leave and I was ready to part with her, but seeing I was bent on staying another day she changed her mind. The town didn't seem so bad that morning. The people seemed to be a mixture of races; gypsies and Arabs, as well as Spanish and European.

Back at our hotel, we asked about a tour schedule and were told that most of the tours were done very early in the morning. Since it was later in the day, by the time we inquired, the next thing was to find out how much a cab would cost. We found a cabbie who would take us to the Alhambra and wait for us as well as give us a tour of the city for 3000 pesetas. I did some arithmetic and found that we could afford the price and he was hired. That turned out to be a very good deal for us. We got to visit the Alhambra and the surrounding attractions and gardens. We made it back to the hotel ready to have our dinner and relax a bit before retiring. My desire to see the subject of the song "Granada" was fulfilled. Granada had been what I expected and more.

The next morning was July 6th, and the middle of the week. We packed our bags after breakfast, paid our hotel bill and were off to the train station, where we had a long wait before boarding the train. This time we would be off to Valencia, the theme of a song which made me think of that city as "romantic." The train was very crowded and all the seats in our compartment were reserved. Aside from me and Licel, our company was a lady on her way to Barcelona, a man and his young son, and another man who got on the train a few stops after us. We introduced ourselves to each other and related what our trips were about. Before long we found a bit to talk about and conversed till about 2:00 AM. Suddenly we were in Valencia and we had slept very little. It was still dark when we got off the train and we wondered about what we should do next. For the time being we found a corner in the station to sit and wait for daylight. As soon as daylight came I went out to find a hotel. I found one not too far from the station and immediately got a room for the day. Then I ran back to the train station for Licel and our luggage. Once in our hotel room we settled in and fell asleep for a couple of hours.

After a good rest we were ready to get out and look about the town. We had breakfast as we always did before any sightseeing. All this traveling made us hungry for food, as well as for taking in all the sights. There was an old fort with many monuments, which we did not recognize. As we continued our visit, we came upon a monument to

Cervantes, as well as some very old churches. We also looked for souvenirs to buy, but we may have been in the wrong part of town, because there were not too many interesting shops in that area. Since our money was running low we had to stop at a bank to replenish our cash. The one thing I enjoyed in Valencia was the many orange trees everywhere. Outside of that, this area was in a state of rebuilding and renewing, which was the reason many shops were closed. Back at the hotel we rested and packed for the next day's journey. I was sorry that we did not have the time to see more of Valencia, but we had to keep moving. We left with that song still running through my head and heart.

It was Friday, July 8th, when we caught the train out of Valencia, and were off to Barcelona on the new and streamline train, the Talgo. The ride was beautiful and smooth all the way to Barcelona. We had been warned about Barcelona by different people. "Be careful!" "Watch your purse!" and so on, so we were ready for anything. While on the train we had 1st class seats to ourselves for a while, then at a little town just past Valencia, a couple got on the train. They were from Mexico visiting the husband's family in Spain. We introduced ourselves and conversed on what we had seen so far and why we were visiting Spain. Before long the couple decided to go to the dining car for lunch. We had had lunch before boarding the train so we declined the offer to accompany them. When the couple returned the woman was beside herself. They had heard some of the bad stories about Barcelona. She was really frightened and we became concerned. When we arrived in Barcelona they invited us to stay at the hotel they were staying at, but we thought that it might be too expensive. I had a hotel in mind, but as we were discussing all this the porter overheard our conversation and immediately recommended a place to us. He said that the hotel he recommended was a very fine place. He took the couple to their cab and called a cab for us. He gave the cabbie an address and we were off to our hotel. We were brought to a loud and crowded place called the Ramblas. The hotel itself seemed like some sort of an old beat up building. It was not the fine place the porter had said it was. It did not look like a regular hotel. It looked more like a dive, but it was getting late and we thought we would give it a try. We were shown our room which was messy and had broken shades. All together the whole ambiance looked unhealthy and unsafe. It was a sleazy hotel, but we had no choice by now, since it was already far into the afternoon, and we were tired and hungry as well. We decided to make the best of it and stay the night, making sure our door was locked, and to leave first thing in the morning. Before retiring that night we called the hotel we had chosen earlier to make our reservation for a room the next day. Having made up our minds, we went out for dinner and shopped a bit clutching our purses. That night we got ready for bed but never got to sleep until late in the night. It was hard to sleep because down in the courtyard was a grand party going on. There was a band playing, guitars strumming and people singing and dancing Spanish and gypsy dances far into the morning. Licel and I took turns trying to sleep and yet we enjoyed seeing all the gaiety going on down in that vast plaza from our window. However, we soon fell asleep in spite of the noise and were up very early to check out of this house of ill repute. That was what we felt this place to be, after seeing what kind of people went in and out on a certain floor. In spite of being so tired, we were up and out of that place with the rising sun. We took a cab to a real hotel,"Hotel Paseo de Gracia" and waited till it was time to check in. Again we went to bed to catch up on our sleep. Later we called the couple we had met on the train to thank them and let them know that we were alright and wished them the best. Now we could relax and get to do some sight-seeing with ease. We took the Metro and a bus to an artist show in a place called "the Spanish Village," where artists from most every province entered their specialties. On our way to another art exhibit, we ran into our classmates who had made it to Barcelona. We got to see each other and compare notes, then parted. After two days in this town we had done some shopping and seen a few interesting sights. It was time to leave Spain and start back to France. Having bought some gifts, we had some real packing to do. I wondered if I would ever see Spain again. We left Barcelona with the wish that we would have loved to see more, but enjoyed what we could with the time we had.

It was Sunday, July 10, 1983. We were up early, paid our hotel bill and quickly were off to catch our train. We were tired and tried to sleep most of the way to the border, but it was a restless sleep. Arriving at the border of Spain and France - La Tour, France - we saw that the train on the French side was getting ready to leave. We quickly waved to the porter and signaled him to please wait for us. He waved back to us and called out to us in French. "Vite, vite "he cried. We in turn called out to him "Attend, attend." In short we were calling to the porter to please wait for us, and the porter was calling us to hurry. We made it just in time.

BACK TO FRANCE

We were leaving Spain and on the way to Toulouse, France, where we would spend a day before taking the overnight train to Paris. In Paris, we would be spending another two days, where it was imperative that we make the most of our time. However, on the way to Toulouse, it was necessary to rest and try to keep as cool as possible on that very warm day. On arriving in Toulouse, we checked into a hotel, and after all our settling of beds and drawers we went to find a place to have dinner. By that time we were tired and hungry. After dinner we tried to relax a bit before retiring. The next morning we went down early for breakfast before going to the bank, then to the travel agency to confirm our airline reservations for our return flight to the USA. With all that out of the way, the next thing was to make our reservations for the overnight train to Paris the following day.

On Monday, July 11th we checked out of the hotel and had put our bags in a locker at the train station, which was something we could never do in Spain. For the rest of the day we wandered about the town and spent the time going in and out of shops looking to see if there was anything that might interest us. After all this wandering about, we found a park bench in a shady spot, where we finally sat down to rest. Below the park benches was a grassy knoll with trees here and there. We had been resting a few minutes when a lady came by, flipped her jacket down beneath a tree, and lying on her jacket she fell asleep. Ten minutes later a fellow walked over to another tree and did the same thing. Having my pad and pencil handy I decided to sketch them.

Illustration 2: SLEEPING IN THE PARK

We eventually left that place, went back to the station, where we again wandered a bit before going to the cafeteria for a snack. Soon, it was time to get our packages out of the locker and be ready to board the train. That evening we found our place on the train and made ready to sleep on our bunks. We arrived in Paris about 6:30 AM, and were somewhat rested. The couchettes were not like our own beds, but they were better than trying to sleep on the seat of the train. On arriving in Paris, we had to wait till noon to get into our room at the hotel. Noon seems to be the hour when new occupants check in and old ones check out. Once in our room, we did some washing of our clothes, and checked the time that the Louvre Art Museum would be opening. It was now July 12, 1983. We would be going to Brussels in two days. I decided to make the most of my time left in Paris. I did not want to go wandering around by myself, but I was going to take advantage of the days left one way or another. Licel could not make up her mind on what she wanted to do on these last days in Paris. However, she eventually did give in to going and doing what we could. That evening we had dinner and wandered around the area for a while before getting ready for the night's rest.

The next day it was most important to get to the Louvre. After our breakfast, we did just that. It was great to revisit the Museum. We got to see so much that we had not seen before. I visited with the Mona Lisa for a few minutes and many other wonders. After that we went back to the hotel to rest and get ready for the next day, which would be our day to depart for Brussels. Licel and I decided to take a walk outside just to see what might be going on. Our hotel was next to the Sorbonne where we noticed there was an activity going on. We peeked through the window to get a glimpse of what was happening. One of the teachers saw us and came out to see who we were. When we told her we were from the hotel next door, she invited us to come in and to enjoy the play. We thanked her kindly and excused ourselves, apologizing for the intrusion.

That night we slept lightly because of the constant fireworks going off almost the whole night for Bastille Day. We slept till 8:30 AM, then were up to finish packing our belongings, had our breakfast and were off to the train station. We had our luggage sent to the Brussels "gare midi", the train station in Brussels. On arriving to the Brussels train station we had to wait for our luggage. Once our luggage arrived we made our way to the airport, where we then had to wait till the next morning to board our plane for the states. That night I called home and was so happy to hear my husband's voice. He was making dinner for my sister and her husband, who would be there when I arrived back in Chicago. It had been a great and wonderful experience, which I would never forget, but it would be great to be home again.

MY ADVENTURES IN SOUTHERN FRANCE

In the Gironde region, about 60 kilometers southwest of Bordeaux, is the small town of Arcachon, which is located on the southern point of the Arcachon Basin, off the Bay of Biscay. The population there is approximately 16,000. In the older section of the city, there are narrow streets with narrow walks built of stone, but in the newer section, there are beautiful wide streets with regular type walks. In some areas the old streets somehow run into and blend with the new ones. The city is divided into two sections. One is "la ville d'hiver," where the residents live all year round. There, great pride is taken in the upkeep of the homes and their surroundings. Homes are well built and made to withstand all of the seasons. The other section is called "la ville d'ete." These are the houses near the beaches and hotels, which are rented out all summer, or a greater part of the year. Many of the homes are southern chalet style and most have real tile roofs. Then there are the estate homes, which are built in the style of small castles. Plants abound surrounding every home, regardless of yard area.

In the center of the city is the business area. There one finds a large open market with its great assortment of eating options, from fresh fruits and vegetables, to freshly caught fish. One can also find a great variety of small shops lined up and down every street in the business district. Cafes, where a person can stop for a little rest and refreshment, are scattered among all the other shops. Arcachon has its share of specialty shops such as "patisseries" or bakeries. There are quite a few of these, almost one on every block. Each patisserie has such a great variety of fancy and exotic looking pastries that a person could ponder for hours trying to make the desired choice. There is also an area consisting of coffee and tea shops, as well as fine gift shops for those special purchases. The Mono Prix is the French version of a cross between a Jewel Food Store and a K-Mart. It is also located in the shopping center of town.

For all this access to buying and shopping, one had better get out to shop early and have a good breakfast because exactly at noon all shops close till 3:00 PM. Dinner is not served anywhere till around 7:00 PM. Away from the central shopping area, one finds other specialty shops which sell goods like small groceries or self-services. Though the commercial part of this area does well, the industry of Arcachon is rather limited.

Tourism is one of the revenue sources for the little town of Arcachon. The stretch between Bayonne and Arcachon has been named the silver coast because of the silvery sands making up the beaches. The weather in this area is warm and comfortable most of the year, with only a short spell of cooler weather during the extreme winter. This long stretch of beach is one of the main attractions during the summer months when daylight saving time is pushed ahead, not by one but by two hours, to stretch the daylight all the way to 10:00 PM. Tourists have the choice of staying in one of the numerous hotels along or near the beach, or renting a house or apartment in the" ville d'ete." Besides the beaches, the other attraction in Arcachon and nearby are the unbelievable sand dunes of Pyla. These are a long stretch of sand hills as high as 117 meters. On the one side it slopes down to the sea and on the other side it slopes down into a forest. For centuries, masses of sand have been deposited along the coast of this region by the currents of the Gironde estuary carrying sand and silt, thus building a stretch of Dunes along Pyla. Because the blowing winds push the sand to the West, bogs and marshes have formed. For this reason the planting of many pines and oaks was undertaken. Today there are vast forests of pine and oak which serve to stabilize the soil of the sandy dunes. These forests also make paper mills and barrel making possible in this area. Another important occupation of the region is the oyster culture, where silt deposits make for fine oyster beds.

If anyone enjoys watching a game of pelot Basque, there is a court where the game is played on the weekends. Another of the favorite sports on the dunes is the glider plane. Of course, no town in France can be complete without its casino. The casino is the place where many important events are held. There always seems to be entertainment and laughter inside. Of course, there are fine and mediocre restaurants in different parts of town. Many of the hotels also serve dinners as well as continental breakfast. For gift shopping there are many exotic shops just off the beach near the hotels. Last but not least, Arcachon has a museum-aquarium, a beautiful library, a park and beautiful flowers everywhere. There is also an old church which chimes each hour and a half, all day and night.

The people of Arcachon, I cannot say for sure, are fine or stern, friendly or unfriendly, for I had limited contact with only a few people in the time spent there. The people I had the pleasure of meeting were indeed fine, friendly and helpful. In every shop I visited, I did my best to ask a question or two, which inevitably evoked an answer and a conversation would ensue. Such was the case with the good madam at the post office, the good sir making mattresses by hand, the lady at the tea shop, la cordonniere*, the baker's wife, and the cashier at the epicerie**. But of all the people I met and enjoyed conversing with, I fondly remember Olivier and his father, and Madam and Mr. Dagault. Maybe it was because I got to know these fine people a little better. We spent a little more time together and discussed more subjects, therefore making for better understanding.

All in all it was a great and enjoyable experience and a never to be forgotten vacation with all the friends I met and places I visited in France.

la ville d'hiver----------------a winter village

la ville d' ete------------------summer village

la cordonniere*-------------shoe repair attendant

epicerie**--------------------groceries store

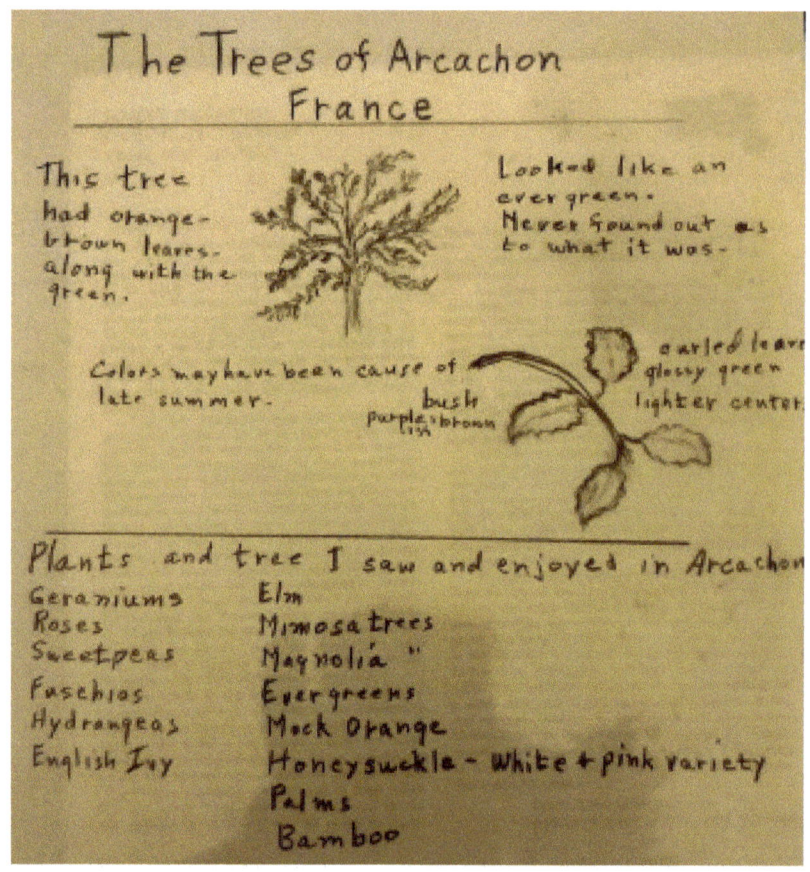

Illustration 3: TREES OF ARCACHON FRANCE

OUR TRIP TO MEXICO IN THE YEAR 1979

We arrived on Saturday, December 29, 1979 in Mexico City. On our first day after settling down in our hotel we went on a city tour offered by the hotel, which consisted of the Government Presidential Palace, the Zocalo and the Anthropological Museum. We also rode the Subway System that day. We decided to take the tours offered by the hotel, since we did not know which would be the best attractions.

This was going to be a challenging trip. Ig had suddenly decided that he wanted to meet my family in Mexico. I was not sure how he would take to this trip since we had never been in Mexico together, but here we were and I held my breath. But before going to meet my people we took on the hotel tours.

On Sunday, Dec 30th, our 2nd day in Mexico City, we went to the Ballet Folklorico in the morning, which was beautiful and very enjoyable. Next it was to Zochimilco (the Floating gardens) in the afternoon which to me was a disappointment. The boats were beautifully decorated, but the ambiance was not what I expected. Next was a visit to the University grounds, which was interesting. In the afternoon we went to the bullfights and being from the USA, I did not really take to that form of entertainment. Our morning guide was a real character – a cross between Geronimo and Al Capone, or maybe Long John Silver and One Eyed Jack.

On Monday, Dec. 31st, we were given a new guide. Victor was our guide for the day and he was a gentleman. Getting in the car, we saw the same people we had met twice the day before on our tours. After recognizing each other on the third day, we introduced ourselves and soon we looked for each other on all our outings. They happened to be in a hotel just down the street from ours.

The first item of this day was a visit to the Shrine of Guadalupe, which was up on the hill called Tepeyac, then to the church where the cloak is on display. Next was a long ride through the city and out to Teotihuacán and the Pyramids. That was spectacular. The pyramid of Teotihuacán was, to the ancient Mayans, the Pyramid of the Sun and the Temple to Quetzalcoatl, an ancient Mayan god.

We rented a car when we made the arrangements for this trip, and today was the day to pick it up since we were planning the big trip to see my family the next day. We had gone on all the hotel tours and now were ready to make the trip we had planned. A visit to my family members in the hills of Guanajuato. But for that night we would be going to the New Years Party being hosted by the hotel.

That evening we enjoyed a formal dinner and were entertained by a singer, Roberto Vander, and a mime act. Both were very entertaining. The orchestra played some very familiar tunes as well as beautiful old ones. We shared our table with a couple from Texas, with whom we discussed several subjects, but agreed on few. This was how we welcomed the New Year in 1980, on our fourth day in Mexico City.

Early in the morning we checked out of the hotel and were on our way to Queretaro, the town where Maximilian met his fate. The sun felt so good in the cool morning and the road was practically ours alone. There was very little traffic on this New Year's Day. We reached Queretaro about 1:00 o'clock in the afternoon and checked into the Holiday Inn. We then decided to get on the road to Guanajuato. Since it was already well into the afternoon we wanted to get our visit out of the way early so that we could get back to the hotel before dark. Before too long we reached the road to the big town of Celaya. We kept to the main road and eventually reached the small town of Tamayo's Corner or Rincon de Tamayo, where there was a celebration going on, probably a New Year celebration, but we were looking for the road to the village called Canoas. On leaving the town we followed the map and were now heading for a village up in the mountain. The road going up the mountain got somewhat narrow and turned into a dirt road for a short way. Then we came upon a cobblestone road leading us up to the mountain community.

Before long we found my uncle's house. It was so good to see him and my cousin. While we were there he took us around his land. When we got to a Cactus plant he cut off a beautiful purple cactus pear, cleaned it, peeled it and cut it in half. He gave me and Nacho each a half. We took our halves and looked at each other as if to say, 'is it safe to eat?' The hesitation lasted a few seconds, then we decided to throw caution to the wind and down the hatch they went. The fruit was absolutely delicious.

Too soon we had to leave since we did not want to be too far from our hotel in the dark. We promised to come back the next day and said our goodbyes. The next day, after a serious discussion, we decided to drive back to my uncle's house for a short while. The whole family came to see us, so we took pictures before we left. Next we went to my cousin's house in town to see my city cousins. For a short while we waited for my aunt, then started out to buy something when we ran into her. She was on her way to my cousin's house to see us. We greeted each other and soon we were back at my cousin's house. We visited together for a while until it was time to depart before darkness.

After visiting with my family for those few days, it was time to go back to Mexico City to make arrangements for our return home. It was the New Year weekend and the town was buzzing with festivities, parades and the like. Nacho wanted to stay in the hotel to watch the Bears on our final Sunday. I explained to him that we were in a place where we might never return. I thought we should go to the museum while we had the time, then go to dinner. I finally convinced him and we were on our way.

The museum was very interesting, with exhibits of many historical items and their history. The time passed quickly and before long the museum was about to close. I found Nacho deeply engrossed in several exhibits. All in all he enjoyed the excursion and was very interested in much of what he saw, but now it was off to dinner and we were really hungry.

MY LAST TRIP TO MEXICO

Our plane landed in Leon, Mexico in the afternoon. My travel companion was my daughter Gloria. After searching for the person that I thought would be there to pick us up, I realized that that person had never made it to the airport. Now it was up to us to figure out how get to our destination, which was a small town that was several miles from the airport. We finally decided, with reservation, to hire a cab to drive us the distance.

We got to my cousin's house and were very thankful to have arrived safely, even though the price of the taxi seemed a bit high. All things considered, it was worth it since we were safely and happily together with my relatives. We spent a full week with my cousins, Raquel and Francisco, where we were welcomed and made to feel at home. While there, we slept in one of their bedrooms, ate whatever was cooked, and did our best to be helpful. We wanted to be cooperative as much as we could, but were not permitted to intervene too much. Actually, we were treated as a guest and not relatives, so we just enjoyed being pampered.

My cousin Raquel and I are daughters of two sisters. We have that in common, and we understand each other. She is much younger than I am, and although she never learned to read or write, that never held her back. She knew how to take care of her family, and had interests in friends and whatever was going on in the community. She also knew how to handle both Mexican and American money. She had a busy life with family and many friends.

Gloria and I spent the week wandering and looking around. I enjoyed observing all the plants in their yard, and watching their chicks in the compound. Aside from that I was also trying to understand the so called "futball" that Francisco watched daily, when the little ones were not watching cartoons. Raquel tried to have something to eat constantly and she tried to please us as much as she could. We tried to be good guests and let her know that we were fine with whatever she did.

At some point I thought I should let them know that I had written a book. When I tried to show it to them, they did not seem interested, so I put it away. Before long my other relatives came by to greet us. Among them was my cousin Nelia, whom I had known since I was very young. She was closer to my age. It was a great joy to see her again! We talked and laughed about distant memories of our pasts. Visiting with my cousins was something I had been longing to do. Knowing that I was at a point in my life where I was getting older made this visit even more special.

I decided that to make the most of my trip to Mexico that I should try to see as much of my family as possible. For this I had to make arrangements to go into the town of Celaya. I thought I might use the public transportation, but my cousin, Nelia, made it clear that she was ready to help me get to wherever I wanted to go. Thus we made arrangements to go to Celaya the next day, for which I was thankful, since I did not remember how to get there. My cousin showed up early in the morning and after our coffee and breakfast we left. We walked to the corner and waited for the bus that would take us into town. We did not have to wait too long before the bus arrived. We boarded and soon we were on our way to the city of Celaya. When we reached the town, I did not recognize any part of a city I once knew. It was totally shocking to see that the town had changed so much. It was filled for blocks with stores, shops, and stands of one kind or another. I knew that there was an area set aside for business, but now it had grown to the point that neighborhood houses seemed to have disappeared. At least that was my impression, since I had not been there for such a long time. I was surprised to see that so much change had taken place.

When we arrived at my other cousin's home we were greeted and greatly welcomed by the family. I felt that they were all as happy to see me as I was to see them. We greeted each other with many hugs. We were made to feel very welcome. Soon we were invited to have lunch, which was prepared during all the getting acquainted with the family members I had not met. While we were having lunch, I asked many questions about family things. After lunch, I thought I would show the family the book I had written. They all seemed very interested and asked me many questions. This made me feel very much appreciated. We had to leave before it got dark and it seemed like it was too soon. As we parted I felt a sense of regret, knowing that I would not be able to get back to the Celaya to visit with that part of my family a second time.

The next day my cousin Raquel took Gloria and I shopping. She showed us the neighborhood, as well as introduced us to many of her friends and neighbors. She knows just about everyone and her errands generally take twice as long because she and the neighbors love to discuss this and that. We went to a little store where she did some shopping, but also introduced us to the keeper, who was very friendly. We discussed many things of interest about our different lives.

The next interesting visit was with the next door neighbors, who were an older couple. Having several cows on their property, they were in the milk business. The man milked the cows every morning and then sold the milk. This man himself turned out to be a distant relative of my father's family, as our conversations revealed, which I found to be so interesting.

The next visit was with a neighbor on the main road who had a large array of different kinds of plants. It was so beautiful to behold. This was a lady who also raised pigs. She had about eight or ten pigs in their pens, and one of them had just had babies. The little piglets were already wandering a bit and the mother pig was very watchful. All this was so interesting to me since I had never seen wonders like these. I was fascinated by it all. My cousin really had some good neighbors.

Two days later, our week's visit was over and it was time to leave Mexico. A distant relative was asked if he would do us the favor of driving us to the town where the airport was situated. My cousin Raquel and her husband accompanied us on the long ride for which we were very grateful. On the way we talked of many things. We passed so many points of interest, one of which was a beautiful range of mountains which I wished I could have had the time to visit and enjoy.

It took us over two hours to reach the airport only to find that our flight was delayed for at least two hours. My cousins and I visited a bit more, but since it would be a long time before the flight departed, they decided to leave in order to get back to their home before dark. So we hugged, said our goodbyes and they left, leaving us alone to wait for our turn to board the plane.

We checked our luggage in and questioned the attendant as to the time and place to be ready to board the plane for the flight. It was a long wait. We had to keep checking as to when we could get into the proper line. Eventually we boarded and were on the plane to Chicago. Once in my seat, I suddenly had a runny nose which would not stop and made me most uncomfortable. I struggled with this discomfort for the whole trip back. When I arrived in Chicago, I went to retrieve my luggage, but it never came. Aside from waiting for my luggage, I also tried to find my son who was hopefully there and looking for us. He was going to take us home, and it was a while before we found each other. Once we were together we waited for my luggage, but it never came.

I was totally frustrated and tired. Before leaving for home I had to fill out forms and give my address and whatever information was needed to eventually get my luggage to me. It was four o'clock in the morning by the time I made it home. What a night!! I enjoyed the visit with my relatives, but the long wait before my departure, the irritation during the flight, and then losing my luggage, made for a very unpleasant return trip. I hoped I would never have to repeat that part of any travel experience again.

913 BLUE ISLAND AVENUE

Today there is no such address—no such building. In its place is the University of Illinois Chicago Campus. But at one time it was a very vibrant and lively place. 913 was the address of a series of buildings, called a complex. Each building housed about five or six families. We lived in flats which today are called apartments.

Blue Island was neither blue or an island. That was just the name of this diagonal street in Chicago. The street itself was not a busy street. On our block there were three separate buildings with businesses on the street floor. It was a short block and it was not crowded with many buildings or houses. The ground floor of our building had two store front spaces. One of them was a nut shelling shop, which was on our side of the complex. I'm not sure what the store on the other side of the complex was but it always seemed empty.

The landlord, whom I think owned or leased the whole building, was Mr. Cava. He was a rather stout man with a very good disposition. His wife was on the heavy side and spoke very little English. They had two daughters and three sons. The daughters were Theresa and Philomena. Theresa was not very friendly and, for the most part, was not interested in speaking to or dealing with the tenants. Every now and then she would have a tiff with her mother and would scream at her, not caring if anyone heard their strife. A few times I heard her tell her mother to "go to hell" at the top of her lungs not caring who heard. This would ring up and down the hall, but no one ever looked out to see the outcome. Philomena was the opposite of her older sister. She was a very pleasant girl, a little on the heavy side, but was always smiling and loved talking with the tenants. There were three sons, whose names I have forgotten. The sons were always busy and on the go. The younger one was in school and the other two appeared to have jobs. I do remember the middle sons' name, Stanley, because he was handsome, tall, trim and seemed to be very sociable. I had seen him dressed and ready to go on a date or whatever a few times. All of a sudden, I did not see him for a while. When I did see him again, he was in a wheel chair. Philomena would bring him out to the back porch for short periods. He must have come down with some sickness such as MS or the like because after two or three years, he passed away. We had moved to another flat by that time, but I went to his wake and extended my condolences to the family. This is a sad memory.

All the tenants in our building kept pretty much to themselves. Perhaps we would meet a tenant coming or going in the halls, then we would smile or say hello and keep going. We lived on the second floor in a rear flat. The flat above us was similar to ours and was occupied by an older couple from Italy. Their knowledge of English was minimal. They were brother and sister as far as I knew, and both were stout and not very tall. He was Giuseppe and she was Rosa. She had very curly hair which made her face seem rounder than it was. They were a most entertaining couple. They also had a female dog that was named Queenie.

Giuseppe almost always did the shopping for them. Every day he would come home by the back alley, stand in the yard behind the shops of our building and give a whistle to Rosa. She would then lower a basket on a rope for the groceries or whatever and pull the basket up to their apartment. To them it was like a little dumb waiter or an elevator for the the groceries or whatever he had purchased. Some days it would go on several times and occasionally I would watch that basket going up and down from my window. This was one of my interesting and entertaining past times.

Another source of entertainment that went on with Rosa was the discipline of her dog, Queenie. Every day it was necessary to let Queenie out to do her business. While she was downstairs she would take care of her needs, then spend time sniffing around and checking out every corner of the big porch and yard. A few minutes later Rosa would give Queenie the call to come back home, but Queenie would totally ignore her. Queenie's total ignorance would almost make Rosa cry. She would call Queenie over and over again, pleading with her to come up the stairs. Again Rosa would call, begging her pooch in Italian, "Queenie, veni qua, Queenie." Finally after all that begging, Queenie decided it was time to obey and up she would climb the stairs and go back to her mistress. That was quite an entertaining show.

To me, of course, the most important tenants were my family, the Alvarez clan. The Alvarez family was made up of me, my two brothers, three sisters, my mother Martha and my stepfather John. My bedroom was actually an extension of the living room with a sliding door in between. Although the sliding door was there it was never used and may have been meant for some other purpose. Nonetheless, that was my bedroom and study.

John's sister lived in a flat in the building complex next to ours. She lived there with her four children, Adolph, Nadine, Sally, Alice and an adopted daughter Auliria. On warm summer evenings my cousins and I would sit outside on our doorsteps, the front entrance to our flats, and talk and enjoy the evenings. Sometimes, Adolph would play his guitar and we would sing beautiful Mexican songs, harmonizing beautifully. I would be the alto, and Sally and Annie would be the mezzo sopranos. Those were very enjoyable times. Sometimes we would just walk up and down the block with neighborhood friends till almost midnight or until our mothers would call us to break up the visits. It was here that my last sister was born, making us four sisters and two brothers.

It was on the front steps of 913 Blue Island Avenue that Ig and I had many a conversation on many subjects. This was where we got acquainted and began to know each other's histories. This is where I lived after graduating from high school. This is also where I remember having some good and challenging conversations with my mother. It was here that I formed many opinions on life and made many decisions about raising children. Fortunately or unfortunately, those plans never got carried out as I had imagined they would. All in all, I have some very happy memories of 913 Blue Island Avenue.

END OF A BUSY DAY

This particular day had been an extremely busy one. Several appointments had been kept, as well as some very necessary shopping. When I arrived home, I had to fumble for my keys before I could finally open the door. As I walked into the hall of my apartment, I heard the phone ringing. I ran to answer it, but when I picked up the receiver, there was no answer, just a muffled voice, then a click. "Oh well!" I thought, perhaps it was a wrong number or someone playing games. I began to feel rather tired after such a hurried day. I decided that I must get to bed early that night.

I turned the radio on to listen to some music while I proceeded to make my dinner. While cleaning up after dinner, I heard that one of my all-time favorite movies would be showing on the TV after the news. It was against my better judgment to sit up with a late night movie, but it was going to be "Gaslight," with Ingrid Bergman, one of my favorite actresses, and Charles Boyer, my favorite actor, in this good mystery. As tired as I was, I had to watch this suspenseful flick. I made myself comfortable on the sofa, turned the TV on and was ready to enjoy the show. I was watching the movie with full attention, when all of a sudden I heard the squeaking and opening of a door along with the ticking of a clock. On hearing this, I jumped up with dread in my heart, fearing that someone had entered my apartment. Then, I realized that these noises were only going on in the movie, not in my apartment. I had made myself so comfortable that sleep had overtaken my full attention. Now it was time to shut off the television, leave the movie, favorite or not, and get myself to bed for the rest I needed.

JANUARY 1989 – OUR MONTH TRIP WEST

I had been working at West Leyden High School as an aid and tutor in the language department, helping teach English as a Second Language, since 1983. This day, January 19th 1989, was to be my last.

We had acquired a small camper and Ignacio was anxious to try it on a trip across the country. So we made ready and left our Chicagoland home at 4:30 AM on January 23rd. We drove out of Illinois and into Missouri and finally stopped to rest in Joplin, Missouri. Very early the next morning we took to the road again. We drove through Oklahoma, part of Texas and into New Mexico. After all that driving we decided to stop in Grant, New Mexico where we checked into a hotel and had dinner. It was great to sleep in a bed again.

That night it began to snow heavily. That was part of the reason we decided it would be best to stop for the night. There were rumors that the roads would not be passable farther West. In the morning we had breakfast and were getting ready to leave. The snow had stopped and we decided to try getting through in spite of all the snow and rain that had been forecast. However, that was not to be because the camper would not start. What could we do but try to get it fixed? Luckily there was a gas station across from the motel. They took their time and when they got it going they charged Ig a hundred dollars. That of course did not please him because he felt that they could have fixed the problem sooner and for less. He believed that he could have fixed it himself but was at a disadvantage because he did not have the tools and parts needed. So we had to swallow the bitter pill and be on our way.

The road leading the way to Arizona was still snowy and wet so we had to go easy and be patient. Soon we reached Arizona and the roads began to get a little better. Once we reached Arizona we knew we were near our destination. What was our destination? It was Parker, Arizona.

There was some sun but the weather was not warm. The snow on the mountains put a certain amount of chill in the air. Parker is close to the California border. That area had been chosen for what they call "off road racing." When we arrived, there were cars and people everywhere. We were to meet with Henry Omana, Ignacio's nephew. Henry's neighbor was going to be driving a truck in the race. Henry was sponsoring his neighbor's team. So, we all had to find a spot to park our vehicles. In our group we had two campers, a car and the truck that was racing.

These races were held on certain paths in between mountains and over uneven terrain. Also, there were categories of racing vehicles, such as bicycles, motor bikes, different types of cars and small trucks. All of these were painted and decorated in all types of designs, colors and named with logos of whatever the owners could concoct. The name of our contestant was Carlos Urias, the owner of the truck to be raced that day. His co-driver was his son. The truck was painted red and green on a white body. The sponsor's name "Tacos Omana" was boldly painted on both sides and on the back end of the truck. Also on the back of the truck was the number given to this category and the logo "U-B-Ugly." Along with all this, there were other little signs and pictures splashed all over the body of the truck.

Illustration 4: IGNACIO & HENRY OMANA

That Saturday we settled down at the spot assigned to us. The next morning at a given time the races began. Each category was given their time and path to take. It was absolutely unbelievable to see those vehicles racing for all they were worth on this uneven and really rugged terrain. Some drivers had to stop and pull over aside the track to make repairs on their vehicles, while others just went on and made it to the designated finishing point. I was absolutely amazed at all the commotion.

In the meantime, I loved looking at the mountains around us, but the cold air was almost unbearable. It was the end of January and here we were in Arizona. I assumed it would be warm. The sun was out but it did not do much warming. Even though I was wearing layers of clothes and boots, I could hardly keep warm. I could feel the cold all the way to my bones. We had to turn the heat on in the camper in order to have a place to get some of the chill off. In other words, I had never been as cold as I was in Arizona on that day in January. Even in Chicago, where the temperatures fall below zero, I had never felt that cold.

The races went on throughout the day. After the races were over, pictures were taken and prizes were handed out. Ignacio got a photo of himself standing next to the truck. It was all over by late Sunday afternoon, and about that time we headed for Lake Havasu to Henry's house, which was further South in Arizona. It was a great relief to get away from the cold mountains and sleep in a bed again. I finally got a good night's rest. The following day, after a good breakfast, we all drove to Los Angeles. On the way to LA we stopped at a market where we bought some fruit and things for making dinner when we reached our destination. We made it to Henry's house in El Monte, California in the early afternoon. Later that evening Rosette and Edmond, our cousins, came by to see us. We had a good visit with the most important topic of conversation being, "the big races and the bitter cold."

Once in Henry's domain, things began to take on a different character. One of the surprises was a pressing errand that needed to be made to one of his sisters who lived down in San Isidro, which is near the border of Mexico. The next morning we made ready and off we went to San Isidro. We reached Lydia's house late that afternoon. Lydia is Connie's daughter. Connie is Ignacio's older sister and is deceased. At Lydia's we got to meet Connie's other daughters, Luz and Rosie as well as Connie's husband, Henry Sr. We all had a good time talking, exchanging and reminiscing. After dinner and visiting, everyone retired for the night. We were given a master bedroom. The next morning we were invited to Rosie's for breakfast. After some visiting, it was time to return to LA and El Monte.

Once we were back at Henry's, Ignacio and I decided that we should take some time to visit some of our old neighbors who had left Northlake to settle in Los Angeles. One of our old neighbors was Ellen Oeser who had lived across the street from us in Northlake. She and her family had decided to move to California several years back. We paid them a visit, to find that Ellen was a widow, that her daughters were married and that she was living alone. Nonetheless, we visited with her and caught up on all the stories of both our families. We also visited Rosette and Edmond as well as Ig's sister Gloria over the weekend.

The second week of February Henry decided that the guys should go off to heaven knows where. I did not like the idea, but did not want to be a nag, so I just kept quiet. I did say so to Ignacio and could see that he was rather confused about going. He felt that maybe he should trust that it might be interesting. So off they went, Henry, Ignacio, and Edmund. As for me, there I was with Diana, Henry's wife, sort of hanging in the air.

Later that day Barbara, the daughter of Ig's sister Gloria, came over to Henry's and invited me to spend a few days with her. Of course this had been prearranged, so off I went with Barbara. I was glad in a way, because I thought that we would get a chance to talk, exchange stories and get to be good friends. On the first day with her we went to my old work place, Bullocks Wilshire Department Store. That was a sad sight for me because it was not the same place I remembered. All of its elegance was gone. The building had a warehouse look to it and the merchandise was not of the quality I remembered, while the prices were very high. That was a very disappointing visit. The next disappointment was Hollywood and Vine, and the surrounding vicinity. When I was living in LA, back in the 40's, it was an elite neighborhood and shopping area with fine restaurants in the shadow of Grauman's Chinese Theatre. This was another disappointment. What I saw was dirty streets and second hand stores selling junky clothes. Other stores were closed with signs of for rent or for sale. The people walking around in the area were mostly bums and drunks or those on drugs. In effect, vagrants or the like. Only the Grauman's Theatre still looked the same as before. After these disappointing tours it was time to have dinner so we made our way to a steak house. After dinner we went back to Barb's house. Once there she showed me my room which had a big bed, a TV and my own bathroom.

The next day we went shopping. We went to a Nordstroms Department Store and we were there for five hours, or so it seemed. Barb was having a great time trying on suits and shoes of different types and styles, as well as hats to go with the different outfits. Then she had her face made up at the cosmetics section. Finally, after most of the day had gone by, we went to a market to have dinner. We looked at the counter where we could choose what we wanted from a large variety of dishes. We could choose to have a sample of two or three dishes before making a definite choice. We finally decided with certainty as to which dishes we wanted. All this tasting and deciding took at least the better part of an hour. By the time we got our dinner, paid for it, and chose our table, I was famished.

Day 3 was another shopping day. This time it was a shopping spree for purses. Hundreds of purses. She must have tried every purse in the store. She asked which purse I liked and told me to pick one. Every purse I liked she did not agree on. So we were there at least 4 hours before she finally picked one or two. Then it was time to eat again and another one of those experiences like the day before. When we got back to her house, we again went into the same routine. Every evening I thought we would sit together and chat. But to no avail, it was the same each evening. One evening I sat with her in the living room and tried to have a conversation, but she decided she wanted to read the newspaper and was definitely not in the mood for chatting. So off to my room I went and turned on the TV.

On day four we went back to Henry's house, where Diana, whom we always called Chata, was waiting for us. We all made ready for a trip to where, I was not sure. Soon I realized that we were on our way to the border again. Apparently, they knew that we were to meet the men down in Ensenada or Rosarito, or wherever Barbara had her house in Baja. We arrived there in the late afternoon and shortly after, the men showed up. I was greatly relieved to see them back because I worried about Ig. He never wanted to go to Mexico and thought they were going fishing. He told me later that they mostly drank and argued throughout the trip. He was glad when they finally got to Barbara's Gaviotta house. It really was a very nice house, right off the ocean on a hill. It was enjoyable to walk by the ocean. Ig and I did a little walking around by the beach. There were several beautiful homes in the area, all with private security. The homes were mostly occupied by Americans of means. We were there for a couple of days before going back to Henry's.

Once back a big party was planned for Henry and Diana's wedding anniversary. For the party I asked if I could invite my brother and some friends who lived in the area. I was told that I could invite anyone I wanted to the party, so I invited several friends, and my brother and his lady friend. Now I had my cheering section there. This made it more enjoyable for me to have some family and old friends from my home town there. The whole affair turned out to be a lot of fun and a great success. We got to see a lot of the family that we had not seen for a long time. There were those from San Isidro and Garden Grove as well as the children of the cousins. The only family member who did not show up was Ig's sister Gloria. Food was abundant and the mariachi band was very entertaining. A great time was had by all.

After the party, we decided to leave Los Angeles in a day or two. As we were getting ready to leave, Henry and Diana informed us that they wanted to renew their wedding vows in Las Vegas. They asked that Ig and I be part of the "wedding party." So off to Las

Vegas we went. We parked our camper at the Circus Circus Hotel for the time we were going to be in Las Vegas. After taking care of the parking permit and fees we went to meet the others at the hotel they had chosen. A wedding chapel was found and arrangements were made for the wedding. A limo was hired to take us there. The wedding itself took place at one o'clock in the morning. After the ceremony we celebrated by having dinner before going to retire in our rooms. By then I was ready to fall asleep and not that hungry, but we ate anyway. After eating, we went to the casino where Henry doled out $300 to all the members of his wedding party. We were told to gamble or use it for whatever we wanted. I lost my $300 in no time, then felt upset that I had thrown that money away instead of buying some little souvenir. I'll always feel bad about that—a sort of lost opportunity. Finally we decided we had had enough. Henry had also reserved rooms for us so that we did not have to go back to the camper that night. By the time we got to our room to get some sleep it was about 4 o'clock in the morning.

Late the next morning we all got together for brunch. After brunch some went back to Los Angeles, but Ig and I went to Lake Havasu with Diana and Henry. At Havasu we did a little shopping, but mostly rested before heading back to Chicago. A couple of days later we said our goodbyes and many thanks to our hosts and left for Chicago.

I had taken some movies on our way to Havasu, and was doing more of the same as we headed home. On the way back we drove and drove, stopping only for gas and a quick meal. When we stopped in Oklahoma for our next gas and snack, there seemed to be a rather unfriendly atmosphere. I felt uncomfortable. Two men kept staring at us in a very unfriendly way. With an uneasy feeling we hurriedly drank our coffee and left. After that we only stopped for absolute necessities. Ignacio just kept driving, only sleeping when he absolutely needed to, which was not much. Soon we were in St. Louis, Missouri and we began to feel more at ease knowing that we were closer to home. Once we crossed the river we were in Illinois and drove to the first rest stop. On getting out of the camper, I felt cold and reached for my coat, but it was not there. Suddenly I realized that I had left it in El Monte, California. I had forgotten to take my coat before leaving. That made me upset. But I was glad that we were so close to home. We made it safely back to Northlake, and it was great to be home even without my coat.

DREAMS

A Beautiful Song

Dream when you're feeling blue
Dream, that's the thing to do
Just watch the smoke rings rise in the air
You'll find your share of memories there
So dream when the day is through;
Dream and they might come true
Things are never as bad as they seem,
So dream, dream, dream, dream.

A Dream About Ig

I dreamt that Ig and I were walking down some street. With a coat on one arm, I put my other arm around his waist. Somehow I moved over to the other side of him and shifted the coat over and put my other arm around his waist again. We seemed happy. Then we took a train or bus and rode somewhere. We got off and saw a train coming and had to run to catch it. He ran faster and I ran but got there as it was leaving. I climbed on it somehow, but had to start looking for Ig.

End

A Dream About Tom

Tom was a child and we were waiting for the bus. He was wearing a black coat. I told Tom to stay close. As the bus was coming, he ran off somewhere and I had to run after him. I looked for him and called but never found him.

End

IN LOVING MEMORY OF MY HUSBAND IGNACIO

I made cookies one day

Busy hands my only thought

Or so was my intent

A sudden memory of the past

Stole its way into my mind

Making the project sentimental

Yesteryear making cookies was a joy

I'd roll and cut and spoon and press

And into the oven they would go

The kitchen warm and the trays full

The air filled with a tempting scent

Suddenly, I'd hear the cookie monster

Running down the stairs

To partake of the inviting treat

One, two, three and four

Then in between, a gulp of milk

And again and again repeat

I made cookies today

But hear no bounding down the stairs

Once a delight, no more this day

Just the need to share with family

Or with a friend or two

But always the memory lingers on

A TRIP TO THE MOUNTAINS

Last summer we decided to take a trip West. We wanted to see mountains and trails without any guides. It was a time for us to explore the land on our own. What an exciting adventure it would be. We packed our bags and looked at a map to see just where we would start our adventure. We went through Iowa and Nebraska, crossed Colorado where we began to see mountains rising up to the sky. We finally arrived in Utah, which seemed like a place that called out to adventurous people. There, we could see from the road, mountains covered with forest and steep sloping hills leading down to ravines and rapids.

We needed to find a spot with a clearing near the forest to set up our camp. We finally settled on a place near the road next to a small hill. We looked around to determine where we might begin our climb. As we were putting up our tent, two old men appeared from behind the hill. We exchanged greetings, then asked if they knew where would be the best place to begin our climb up to the forest. One of them shook his head and looked at us as if he thought we had lost our minds. According to the old timers, we had better forget that venture because there was danger up in that forest. They told us about one group of adventurers who cut a path up the mountain many months ago. They had cut their way into the forest, but their bones were found later right where we were standing. On hearing that story we thought the matter over and decided to break camp and go back to town. That was our last attempt at bravery.

GOOD DAY FOR A RUN – LITTLE EMOTION

This morning I looked out of my kitchen window and saw the sun shining down full strength on the world. It was like an invitation to adventure. I decided that it would be a perfect day for a long walk along the running path next to the creek. I donned my jogging suit, my cap and my walking shoes, and off I went.

On this particular morning, the path next to the creek was relatively empty. The ducks on the creek were the only ones complaining. The heavier traffic usually started closer to midday. I passed a gaggle of geese, where the male was seriously on guard, while the harem was busy eating. I smiled as I passed them quickly, not wanting to antagonize him. I felt like telling him, don't worry I don't want your girls.

Farther down the path, a boy, who was rather heavy, was exercising at the next station. It appeared that he could barely pull himself up on the bar. I wanted to encourage him but I did not want to stare or embarrass him. I kept moving!

As I was coming to the last station, two young boys were fighting, a short distance from the path. It looked like a serious fight. One of the boys seemed to be getting the best of the other. In fact, there was something like a pleading sound, coming from the receiver of the blows. I almost felt like calling out to them to stop. But then I thought it might make it worse for the boy being punished. My decision was to stay out of it and get on with my business. I figured and hoped that they would stop fighting. I left them wishing they would settle their problems in a better way, and come to some agreement. So I continued on, finished my trek and went home.

MY THIRD GRADE EXPERIENCE

I have many fond memories of my youth. One that stands out vividly is that of my third grade teacher, Mrs. O'Keefe. She was a tall woman with strong but pleasant features and her hair was light gray, almost white. However, the most striking thing about her was her steel blue eyes, which I will never forget.

During this period of time our family moved a lot from one house to another. My school work had gone on fairly well until we moved again. This time we were in the vicinity of a new school, Swing School, where my third grade teacher was Mrs. O'Keefe. She gave us enunciation exercises as well as a period for art. I may have discovered my knack for drawing in her class. I remember drawing a beautiful Easter Lily. Unfortunately, I lost it on the way home from school.

I felt my classes were very interesting and enjoyable, yet somehow I began to lose myself in dreaming, or maybe I was tired for some reason. I became apathetic and my grades began to fall. One day Mrs. O'Keefe requested to see me after school. At this meeting, she explained in no uncertain terms the consequences of my declining scores. I was to have one more chance to right my wrongs. It was made clear to me that I had better get my work up to par or else I would have to repeat third grade. To fail and have to repeat third grade was absolutely unthinkable. How could I face my mother and my father with a failure notice? I cried and promised to improve. With this hanging over my head, I was resolved and determined to work toward passing grades immediately. That semester I made paying full attention to my studies a "must," and passed third grade. I will always and forever be grateful to Mrs. O'Keefe for my one more chance.

YOUNG EMILIA

Illustration 5: THE PHAROAH'S DAUGHTER

Illustration 6: SOPH YR IN HS

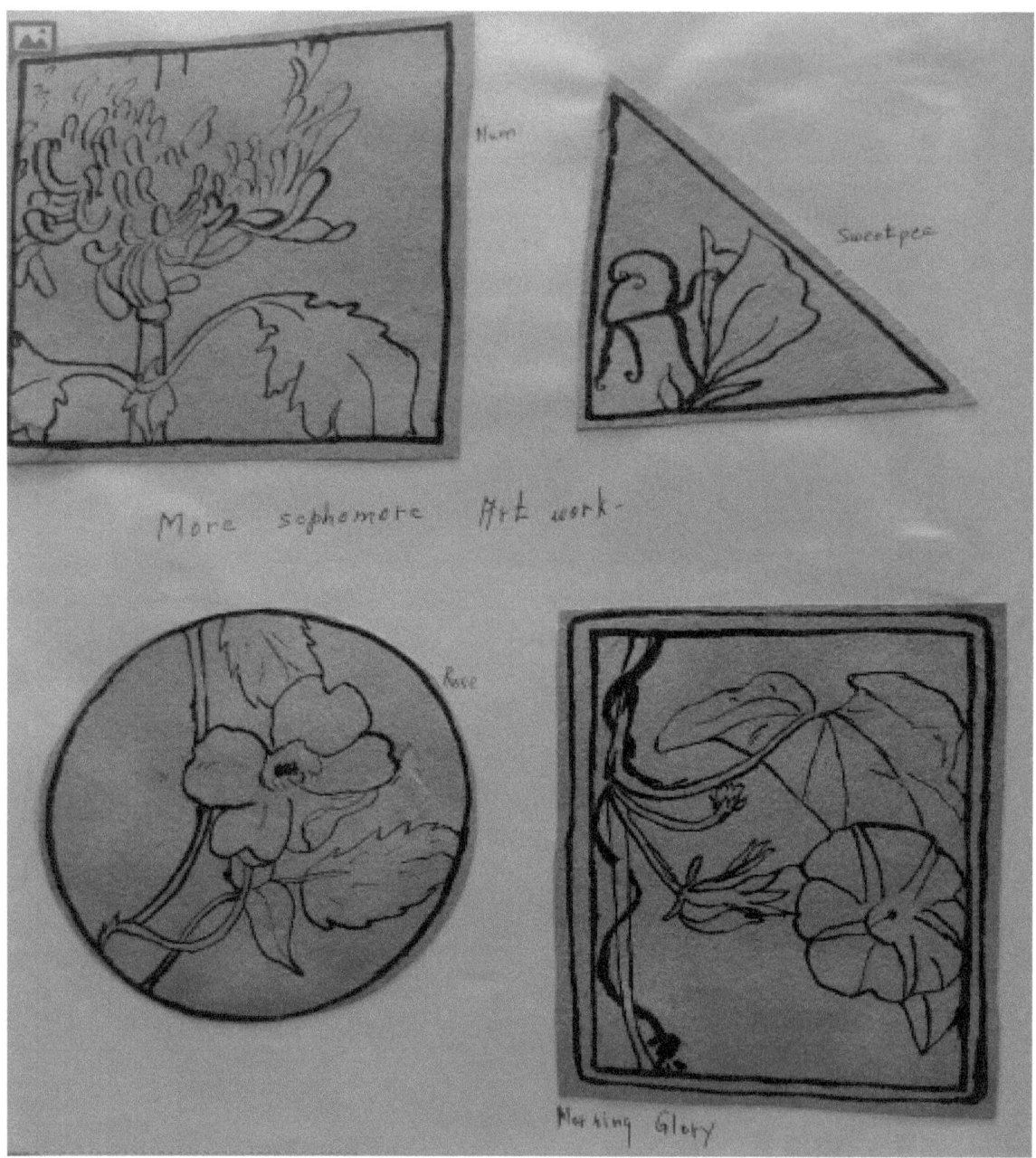

Illustration 7: MORE SOPH ART

MY GREATEST CHALLENGE AS A WRITER

Writing has its challenges. After putting all the notations down on paper, I had to translate what was written into understandable sentences. Then putting my writing in sequence to make proper paragraphs and stories. Going over it all I found that occasionally I had to replace a word here or there with a more meaningful word, as well as correct misspelled words or add left out words. The seemingly never ending process of editing.

But my greatest challenge as a writer has been having the audacity to bring out all those ghosts from the past. Going back in time is a challenge because some memories are painful. Thinking it over, truly the greatest challenge has been facing my past. Looking back at the mistakes I can never correct, the memories which will always be illusive and much that I would like to have done better. However, I feel that I must be brave enough to pass on these stories with the hope that the reader will see some lesson in the written word.

REGRETS REGRETS

As my children grew older, it was inevitable that one by one they would be leaving home in pursuit of their vocations. As the years passed, each one went off with our best wishes, and each one was missed after he or she left. The year came when the first one left for college. One or two years later two more children left the nest. This went on for several years until the time came when the five oldest were off to college or a job. This left the house a rather lonely place to be. The year when all the older children were gone, the house suddenly seemed too quiet, and an eerie emptiness was keenly felt. Only the three youngest children were left with mother and father on our first evening alone. Dad had his shows to watch on TV, so he sat in his special chair and soon dropped off to sleep, as he usually did most evenings. That may have been his way of bearing that lonely feeling.

I, the mother, and my three children left at home all felt the emptiness and absence of those who had left. It seemed the world had closed in on us. Before long each one of us, my three children and I, were sobbing quietly as if our hearts had been broken. It seemed very sad and lonely to face the emptiness in our house. The loneliness the older children had left as they parted, moved us to tears. When I think back on that day I wonder why I, as a mother, could not council the three children left at home, and suggest ways to deal with our lonely feelings. Whatever happened to me that day is something that has always haunted me. I should never have allowed my children to endure those depressed feelings. To this day I wonder what it was that came over me. I just hope that my inability to respond and provide guidance did not have a negative effect on any of my three youngest children. I also hope they will or have forgiven me for my introversion that one time.

REVIEWING LIFE WHILE WAITING AT A LIGHT

It had been over a year since my mate had gone on to the next world, but I still had many moments of reminiscing. Remembering and recalling our life together must be the norm when one loses a partner, especially when one is at home and alone. However, I tried to get on with my life as well as I could. I had put some of my efforts into the continuation of one of my interest, which was ceramics. Now and then, I had the opportunity to put some of my creations on display at different times and at different places. To display my work, it was necessary that I deliver the objects to be displayed to a chosen place, at a specified time. Sometimes I would stay and display my work and at other times I would drop it off. If I dropped it off, on the last day of the show or sale, I had to remember the time to pick up my art work and the money, if any of it had been sold.

It was on one of those days, on the way to pick up my work that I drove off towards the town of Westchester. On the way, the traffic was normal and all was fine. When I reached a main crossing, which was Roosevelt and Wolf Roads, I had to stop for a red light. The pause at that corner brought to mind what Roosevelt Road was to me in my life, and the many events I had experienced related to that road. My childhood family lived on that street at one time. Then there were the many times I used the library on that same street, as well as the many walks taken there, alone or with friends. In short, it was one of many roads, but a main one of my youth. That was the street I was crossing when a young man spoke to me. That same man would become my husband later on. On that road is the hospital where his life ended, and the cemetery where he now lies in eternal rest. I would be passing that cemetery on the way to my destination.

While all this was going on in my mind, I had missed the traffic light change. The light had changed, and for the first time ever, I had to be pulled out of my thoughts by a honk from the car behind me. My time for reminiscing was over and I continued on to the library where my art was waiting to be picked up. I did get home safely and was able to continue on with my day. It just happened to be that that day was Halloween. I never realized it, since I had been in my own world for some time. Then, knocks at the door brought me back to the real world.

EMILIA AT THE ART FAIR

Illustration 8: EMILIA AT THE ART FAIR 1

Illustration 9: EMILIA AT THE ART FAIR 2

Illustration 10: EMILIA AT THE ART FAIR 3

Illustration 11: EMILIA AT THE ART FAIR 4

A LEARNING EXPERIENCE

Thinking back on my youth, I remember many things that I do my best to forget as quickly as they come, because they are unimportant and even foolish. However, now and then some thoughts seem worth keeping. This may be one or the other. I remembered an old favorite song, and began to search for it. I wanted to find it because it brought back fond memories. The song I was thinking of was "Stardust."

After high school graduation, I floundered a bit while trying to decide which path to take to go forward in life. At this time I had a close friend, one with whom I carried on and confided in. She was someone I knew from our neighborhood. We had been in high school together, though she was a year or two ahead of me. After high school she married a guy from the neighborhood and had a baby. We would still get together now and then to chat and discuss the events of the day. It was to her that I related one of my dreams. Some of my dreams were not realistic, as it is with young people. Such was the dream I related to her about signing up for an amateur hour which was taking place in the city. If I could do well at that audition, I could become a radio artist, which might have been one of my bigger dreams. It was about this dream that I confided in her and, as she always did, she encouraged me. On this day I think she thought that my dream was a long shot, and she was probably right, but she supported me anyway. I finally decided to apply to audition at that amateur hour. I began to practice singing the song as much as I could. I was excited, and I rehearsed the song Stardust as often as I could with her as my audience. She would applaud and tell me that I was going to do great. On my last rehearsal she wished me the best. I arrived at the theater on the day assigned feeling that I was well prepared. I was given a number and seated to await my turn. On the stage was a person who played the piano for the contestants. Each contestant had music which he or she gave to the pianist for his or her performance. Little did I know that just knowing the words and tune of a song was not the only requisite. I had no music because I was ignorant of the fact that one needed music for such an audition. I never thought of bringing music for such a popular song, which it was in those days. Soon my number was called. I went upon the stage, told the pianist that I had no music, and asked if she knew the song "Stardust?" After a few seconds of debating she began playing the song. I sang but felt uneasy about not having the music. While singing I realized how unprepared I was. I learned that for an audition like this it took more than just knowing the song. I had to know how to prepare for such an event in order to give a good performance. This happened when I was young, inexperienced and had much to learn.

THE VAGABOND (*ITALIAN*)

taken from a poem by Robert Louis Stevenson

Datemi la faccia dela terra
E la strada davanti a ne
Non cerco amore ne speranza ne ricchezza
Ne un amico che mi capisca
Voglio solo il cielo sopra di me
E la strada sotto miei pied

My translation:
Give me the face of the earth
And the road that spreads before me
Wealth I seek not, nor hope nor love
Nor a friend to understand me
I want only the sky above
And the road below me

Emilia Almada
Lord, grant me strength to meet this day
Please take my hand and lead the way
Teach me to trust and patience too
In daily tasks which I must do
When I falter, hear my prayer
Strength is knowing you are there

WE MOVED TO NORTHLAKE

After the war, it was very hard to find a place to live if you had any children. We had four and one on the way, so for a period of time my husband, my children and I were forced to live with my parents. Something had to change. We began looking for a place to live, either a home or an apartment. After searching for a place to move a family of seven for many months, my husband was told by a co-worker to check out the new city of Northlake. This co-worker had purchased an unfinished house in this new town, and was able to finish it himself. When my husband saw his co-worker's home and realized the low cost of purchasing a shell home, he decided that this was what we needed and could afford. He made the move! He put one hundred dollars down on an unfinished house, learned to use a hammer, and before the following year was over, the house was ready to be occupied. We were on the last street that backed up to the Addison Creek, with one or two houses and many empty lots. Our new neighbors were few and far between. It took a while before we got acquainted. This was where my children were raised.

We moved to Northlake from the big city in the early 1950's. I was a "big city" girl, having been raised in Chicago since I was 3. It was hard to get used to living in a place where I had to drive to a store to do any shopping. The city girl in me was used to having easy access to most anything I wanted or needed. But 50 some years later I did not want to live anywhere but our home in Northlake, IL. The town slogan was, "The City of Friendly People." I had grown very accustomed to that house, that yard and those neighbors. I had hoped to stay there until I had to be carried out to my final resting place.

AFTER GRADUATION FROM HIGH SCHOOL

With my school days over, I began to think about what I should do with my life. I wanted to enroll at Wright Jr. College, but knew that that was not to be. My stepfather was a laborer in the WPA, so our income was minimal and I was the oldest of six children. I did not know about grants or scholarships at the time. Most of my classmates went to work after graduation, with only a few going on to college. In those days, daughters or sons who went to work were expected to help with family expenses. Having no idea as to how to look for employment, I took the summer off after graduation. My mother did not question me about my intentions, however, I did do my best to help with the cooking and upkeep at home. I was given the chore of making tortillas, the family bread, every day. That gave me the feeling that I was contributing a bit.

At that time in my life, I began to let go of some of my shyness and feel some confidence in myself. Summer ended and I felt that I had to get serious about what I should do. Still unsure about the path to take, I began to check ads for jobs and follow leads. Somehow I never got going till the following spring. In the meantime, my mother would give me a dollar here and there for whatever I needed. In the spring I met a lady from our church who hired me to help with soliciting ads from businesses to raise money for the church. That was my first job, which only lasted a week or two, and the pay was not much. My next venture was painting china on the far south side for one dollar a week. I was lucky that the streetcar fare was only seven cents. That job also did not last very long. That dollar went mostly on carfare and lunch. I was barely breaking even. My next job was at a grocery store. There I had to work from eight in the morning till five in the evening. I worked seven days a week in a cold store, for three dollars a week. At least it was within walking distance from home being only five blocks away. The next job I took, because I was desperate, was being a Santa Claus for Christmas. I was a bell ringer for the Salvation Army. My station was downtown in front of the Northern Trust Bank, on the coldest days ever, for four or five hours a day, ringing that little bell. In that spot and at that time, I never expected to see anyone that would know me. Noon came around one day as I kept changing hands and ringing that bell. About then, the workers began coming out for lunch. A young man came out and passed me, then quickly turned around. Recognizing me he remarked, "Is that you Emilia?" I was so embarrassed, I wanted the earth to swallow me. That young man was Joe Moles, the valedictorian of my high school graduating class, who happened to be working at the bank. After that experience, I decided that I was not that desperate.

Next, I tried waitressing, and quickly decided that that kind of work was not for me. Eventually I went to a factory, where I was put on piecework, but because I was a high school graduate, I was soon promoted to filling orders. The pay was also more to my liking. Eleven dollars a week made me feel like a million. With this new employment I began to feel more alive, proud and confident. Now I could help my family and take care of my needs. I had money to spend on whatever I fancied.

Now that I was established in a new job, I began to think about other interests. Because St. Francis church was a poor mission parish, they needed to have a variety of programs in order to supplement their income. For that reason parishioners were recruited to help out by putting on plays and other interesting presentations on special occasions. This caught my interest as well as that of many of the young people in our neighborhood. So with the help of some older members we formed a drama and performance group. We had plays and dancing and singing productions. After the programs, we would have ballroom dancing to finish off the evening.

My mother, along with many of the women of our area, belonged to a civic organization, which had meetings once a month. They also wanted to use our talents for raising money. Along with this, the women also gathered at the Hull House once a week to exchange ideas on the manual arts of sewing, crochet and knitting, as well as just getting together. It was called "The Mother's Club." Children of the mothers also attended these functions but in another area of the building, yet still within sight and sound of the adult area. We played games, did some sewing, knitting and crocheting, or whatever we wanted, all under adult supervision. Sometimes we would make candied apples or cookies, other times we would exchange ideas or just sit quietly and read. It was mostly visiting and fun. This went on at both the Hull House and at the Henry Booth House. They both had the facilities for entertaining children and young adults. One of the young girls in this group was a shy girl named Anna Marie. She was a year or two younger than I, and her shyness was probably due to the fact that she had some pock marks on her face. Other than that she was a nice girl. She almost always stayed close to her mother and did not mingle freely with most of us, unless we were doing something that was interesting to her.

After a year or two in these local activities, I felt that I wanted to dance professionally. I started to take lessons from a fine teacher from California. She had been a pupil of the Cansino School of Dance and I wanted to imitate her form. When I expressed this desire to my parents, my mother was totally against it. She thought it would lead me astray in life. She even had a family friend talk to me, hoping I would change my mind. He explained that there were temptations and dangers that were part of the path I wanted to follow. Once I made him understand that I knew all these facts, and that I would be aware and committed to stay on the right path, he told my mother to let me be on this matter. So, I took my lessons and did some dancing, mostly with the group and at the local church doings. It was all great fun, and I loved the associations and the camaraderie involved in all these activities. But, after about three years of involvement and one year of lessons, I began to slow down and put my mind on other interests. With an awareness of my future, it seemed that dancing might not be what I really wanted for a career. My decision was to go back to school. Also, at that time, I had a love interest.

In the meantime, I heard that Anna Marie had been taking dancing lessons. When I heard that I thought to myself, "She'll never make it." She is not pretty enough and she'll never be able to take the rigors of constant practice. A few years later, to my surprise, I found out that Anna Marie was not only serious about being a dancer, but actually had contracts at nightclubs in Chicago. Along with this, I heard that she had married well. That put me down a peg or two. The shy girl with the pock marked face had reached her star. Proud me had to eat a little bit of crow and admit that I must not have wanted it badly enough. At that point I had to say "cheers" for Anna Marie. Myself, I was still trying to decide what to do with my life.

IS THAT ALL THERE IS

On a beautiful winter morning, I was looking out to the West. At that moment I heard someone on the radio singing the words, "California Here I Come, Right Back Where I Started From." This suddenly made me feel that maybe that was what I wanted to do. Perhaps take a long trip West. My high school days were over and working for a year or two had me asking questions like, "Is that all there is?" Almost every song on the radio seemed to have a message just for me.

DREAMS AND FRIENDS

My high school days had been over for a couple of years and I was wondering where my life would be going. Those were the days when I was trying to decide which road to take. I thought that college would be the best thing for me, but paying for it was a problem. At that time my parents could not afford to pay an extra bill for college tuition. I was going to have to find a job and save for my college education. In the meantime, our neighborhood clubs kept me pretty busy with social activities, as well as some stage performances. A special teacher had the task of directing all that went on, such as dancing, singing and acting. In those days we would put on plays which included singing and dancing. All these activities gave me the idea that perhaps the stage would be my salvation. These activities went on for about two years before things began to change. Some people moved away while others moved on to careers, relationships or commitments. Those were days of wondering what would be the best way to get on with life for many of us. As for me, I decided to take dance lessons in hopes of following my 'performing on stage' dream. The lessons were great for a while, but soon became demanding and tiring. Getting work as a professional dancer was difficult with no guarantees. That dream lasted only a short while. The world was a changing place and I felt I had to keep up or get left behind.

Around that time I recall looking West from my bedroom window. I wondered what the future would bring as my radio played a song I had never heard. This song caught my attention, taking me to a land I had only heard about. The song was about how warm and beautiful it was in California. The words "California here I come, right back where I started from, where bowers of flowers bloom in the sun..." This song made me feel that maybe that was what I wanted to do. I could almost see those bowers of flowers. Maybe taking a long trip would be a good thing. Almost every song on the radio seemed to have a message just for me. That was an option, which seemed wonderful at the time. The dream of going West, at that point in time, was nothing more than that, a dream. But that song planted a seed in me that I hoped might become a reality some day. I knew that I had much work to do to make such a dream come true. I had to get down to business. I had to make my own way in the world. No more depending on my parents to take care of me. It was time to put my dreams away and wake up to the realities of my life.

My parents had been very patient with me because of the great depression. I had been given some chores to do at home, but eventually it was time for me to get a job and contribute financially to my family. I searched for work, but found nothing except a lot of low paying, menial, dead-end jobs. It seemed as if I would never find the right opportunity. I was a high school graduate and all I wanted was something that would stimulate and challenge me. That was the time when the words of the old song kept coming back to me. "Is this all there is?" Would it ever get better? Nonetheless, I had to keep trying to reach present goals and future dreams. The constant search for a good job kept me on the watch. My persistence finally paid off when I found an ad in the newspaper for an order filler position. The company that posted the ad was a well-known business. I applied, passed the interview process, and was hired. I was finally in a position that could open doors to a world I had yet to experience. My duties kept me busy and interested in my work. The people I worked with were also helpful and interesting. It was then that I was able to contribute financially to my family, purchase the things I needed and start to save money for my dreams.

At work I was involved with meetings and activities which kept me busy, and didn't leave much time to think about dreams. It was at one of those meetings when I was introduced to a young lady named Jane. She had just been hired, after moving to Chicago from California, a few weeks earlier. Like most new employees, she needed guidance getting started in her job. Needless to say, I was happy to volunteer for that task. After meeting and showing her around, we had to get back to work. The task of guiding her and helping her learn all the important points of her work went well. At lunch one day I asked Jane about California. She told me that it was a beautiful place, with winters not like ours. During the time we spent together we became good friends. One day she explained to me in detail about her trip from California to Chicago. Apparently she and a friend had hitch-hiked all the way. They had arrived safely and without any incident, for which they were thankful. Jane promised herself never to travel that way again. Upon arriving in Chicago, she and her friend decided to go their separate ways. Her friend wanted to continue traveling in search of lost friends. Thus they parted with good wishes for each other.

Jane and I became good friends for a long time. At some point she confided in me that she was saving her money for the day she would go back to California. She had worked and experienced the Midwest climate for more than three years when that day finally came. She had become homesick and missed the family and friends that she had left behind. Even though she had kept up her work and had made many friends in Chicago, she was ready to go back home. Jane took a bus back to California, keeping her promise to herself never to hitch rides again. As she was making preparations to leave, she invited me to visit her in California someday. I promised that I would, after all it was a dream of mine to go there. She had been gone many months and I missed her, but I knew that someday I would go to visit her. Until I could make that trip, I stayed busy keeping up with work, helping my family and my involvement with neighborhood activities. But I never let go of the idea that I would travel West some day. Jane and I were writing to each other on a regular basis. When things got busy the letter writing would become less frequent. Then, the news about an earthquake in California gave me reason for concern. I wondered if she was okay. I decided it was time for action. I had been working with this company for several years, but had not used much of my vacation time. I decided to take a two week vacation. Arrangements were made for two weeks off and no more. I quickly made reservations for a trip to California. I decided to travel by bus, feeling it was a safe option and would give me a chance to see a some of the country. The day of departure arrived and, after all the good wishes, I was on my way to the sunshine state. The trip took three days and two nights. I was glad to have made that choice because I got to see many interesting places. Along with the scenery, our bus driver narrated the history of sites and cities as we passed each. We arrived at our destination on a beautiful sunny day. It was hard to believe that I was in California. My dream was a reality, yet my new goal was to find Jane. I settled in a hotel near the bus station that had survived the earthquake. The next day I began my search.

The first place I looked was where she worked. On arriving there I could see that there had been some damage, but it did not seem serious. It appeared that work was being done to repair the building. The building was not occupied at the time. Next I went to her apartment. I arrived at her address and saw that there had been some damage, but again nothing too serious. I wondered if she had been injured and taken to a nearby hospital. I set about looking for her at different hospitals in the area. I finally found the hospital where she was. She had been there for a few days. Apparently she had fallen, been hurt and needed medical attention. But most importantly she was okay and I had found her. She was told that she was better and would be released the next day.

It was a happy day when we reunited. She did not know that I had arrived in town and had been looking for her. It turned out to be a very happy surprise and reunion. While I was there visiting with her, a young man showed up in her room who gave her another surprise. It happened to be her brother, Jim, who had been away for over a year. Jane was totally surprised and very happy to see him. After I was introduced to him I decided to let them have some time alone together. I went back to my hotel hoping that they would have a wonderful visit.

The next morning she was dismissed from the hospital with a clean bill of health. She had had a good visit with her brother the night before. Jane, Jim and I met at Jane's apartment after her release from the hospital. Her brother had been traveling the country looking for adventure. He confided in us that the time had come for him to settle down and get a job. Jane and I agreed. The young man had been looking into different occupations and had made a final decision. He had found a job and would be starting work the following day. There would be no more roaming for him. He was ready to settle down.

The visit had been wonderful, but the time had come for me to to prepare for my return trip home. My reservation for the return trip back to Chicago had been set for the day after next at 4:00 in the afternoon. We made the best of the time we had left. Jim joined us each day for dinner. On my last evening there the three of us met at a fine restaurant and had a wonderful meal together. My dream trip to California had come to an end, but not without many fond memories.

CHRONOLOGICAL NOTES

1923 –April	We arrived in Chicago. Jose Macario, Martha and Emilia Rojas.
1924-March	John Rojas was born on the 24th.
1926-February	Joseph Rojas was born on the 3rd. I started first grade at Haines School.
1928-April	Sofia Rojas was born on the 9th.
1929-December	Daniel Rojas was born on the 25th.
1930-May	28th was my birthday when my father left us. Moved to Peoria St. in September. Joseph Rojas passed away on October 31st.
1931-February	Daniel Rojas passed away on February 6th. John Alvarez married my mother in spite of His sister Magdalene's opposition.
1932-March	Jessie Alvarez was born on the 9th. This was Sangamon Street near Maxwell Street Behind the Police Station.
1934-January	Joseph Alvarez was born on the 29th. I graduated grammar school in June. John's Texas cousin came to visit. I started high school in September.
1937--	Moved to 913 Blue Island Avenue
1938-June	Graduated from high school and Margaret Alvarez Was born on October 23rd
1939- March	Met Ignacio R. Almada

Illustration 12: MEXICO TO CHICAGO TO IGNACIO

PART II

THE ART WORKS OF EMILIA ALMADA

CERAMICS

BEST OF SHOW

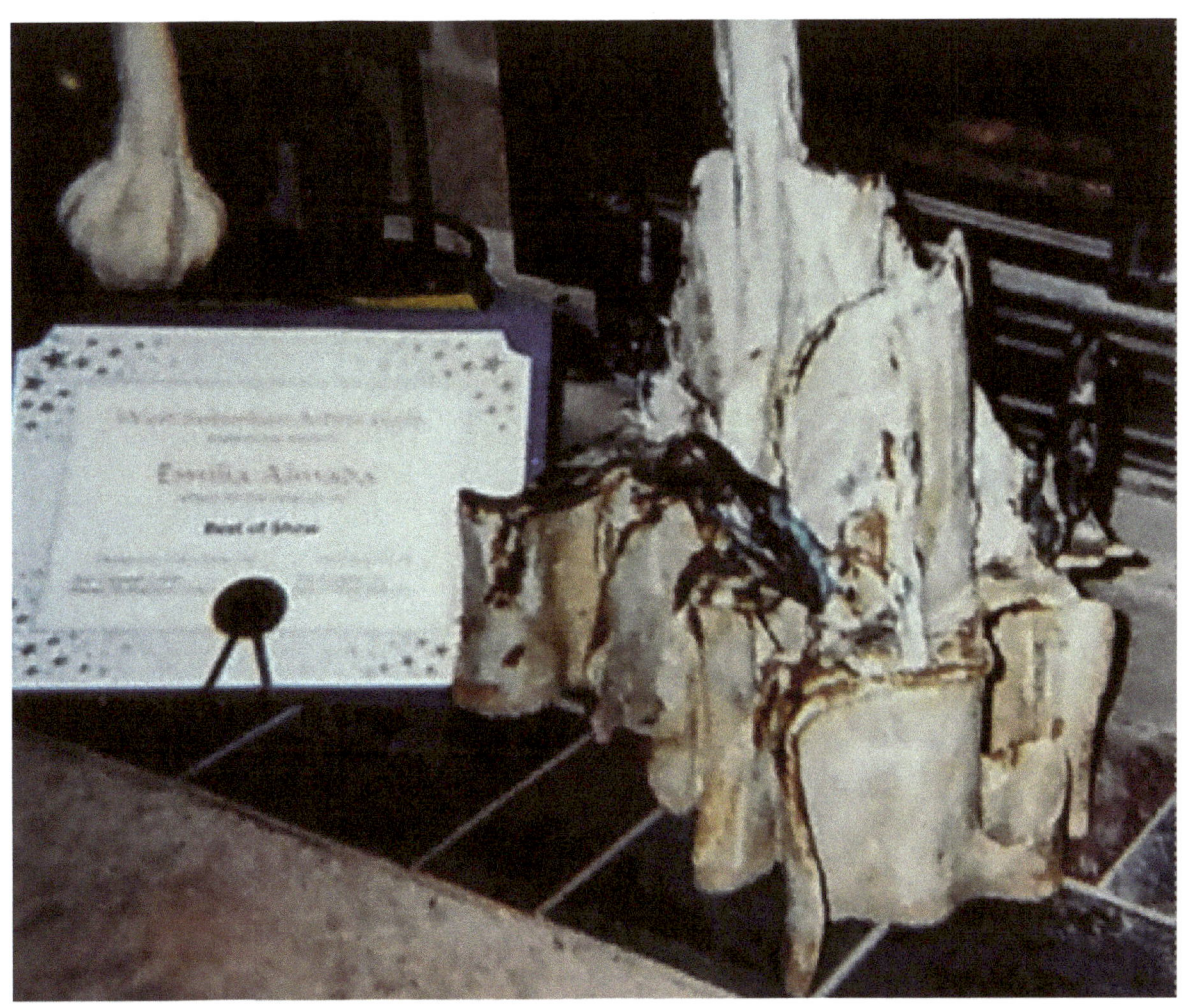

Illustration 13: WHERE WILL THE PENGUINS GO?

Illustration 14: BEST OF SHOW AWARD

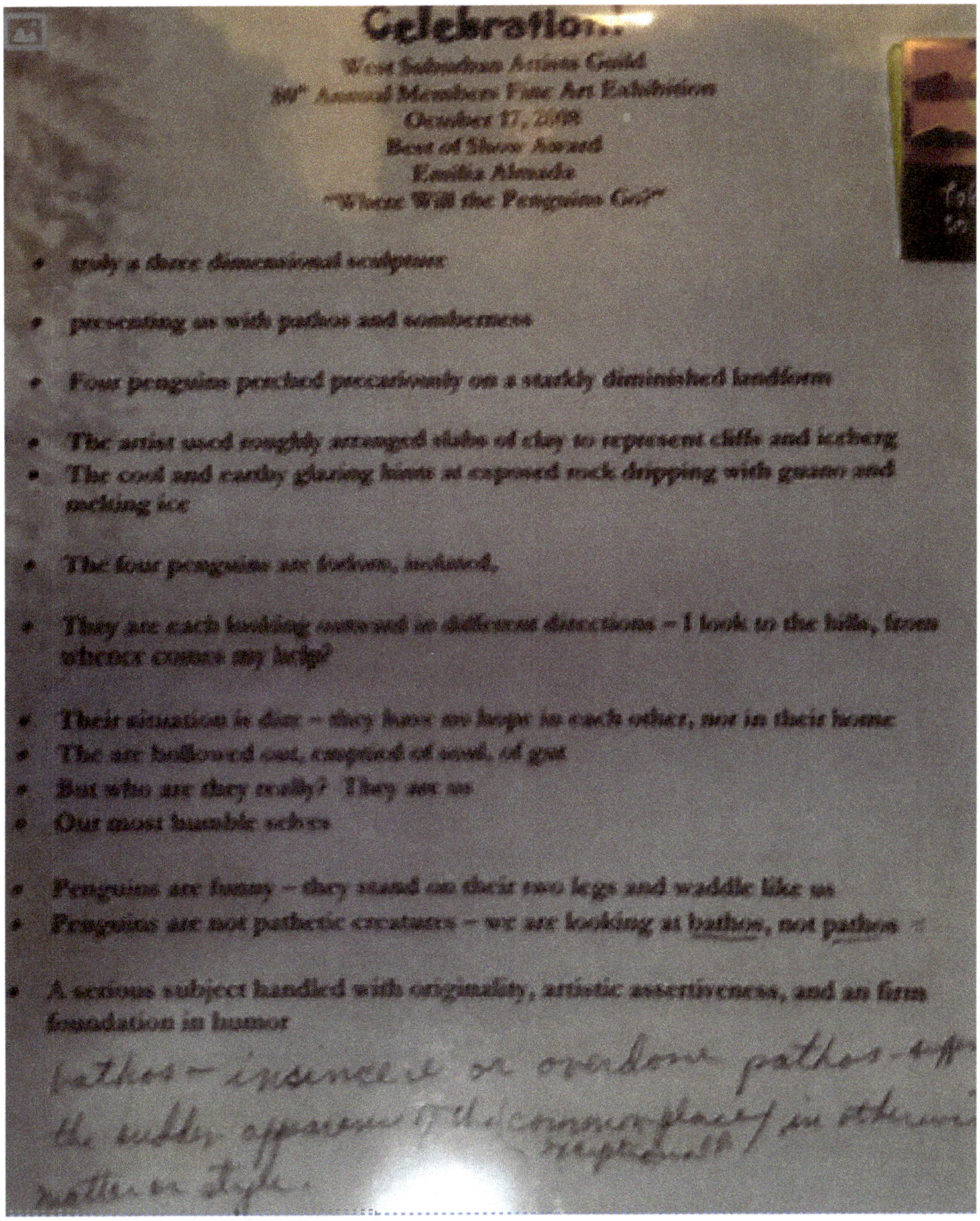

Celebration!

West Suburban Artists Guild

80th Annual Members Fine Art Exhibition

October 17, 2008

Best of Show Award

Emilia Almada

"Where Will the Penguins Go?"

- truly a three dimensional sculpture
- presenting us with pathos and somberness
- Four penguins perched precariously on a starkly diminished landform
- The artist used roughly arranged slabs of clay to represent cliffs and iceberg
- The cool and earthy glazing hints at exposed rock dripping with guano and melting ice
- The four penguins are forlorn, isolated.
- They are each looking outward in different directions – I look to the hills, from whence comes my help?
- Their situation is dire – they have no hope in each other, not in their home
- The are hollowed out, emptied of soul, of gut
- But who are they really? They are us
- Our most humble selves
- Penguins are funny – they stand on their two legs and waddle like us
- Penguins are not pathetic creatures – we are looking at bathos, not pathos
- A serious subject handled with originality, artistic assertiveness, and an firm foundation in humor

bathos – insincere or overdone pathos

the sudden appearance of the commonplace in otherwise

matter or style.

Illustration 15: JUDGES COMMENTS

Illustration 16: BUST OF IGNACIO

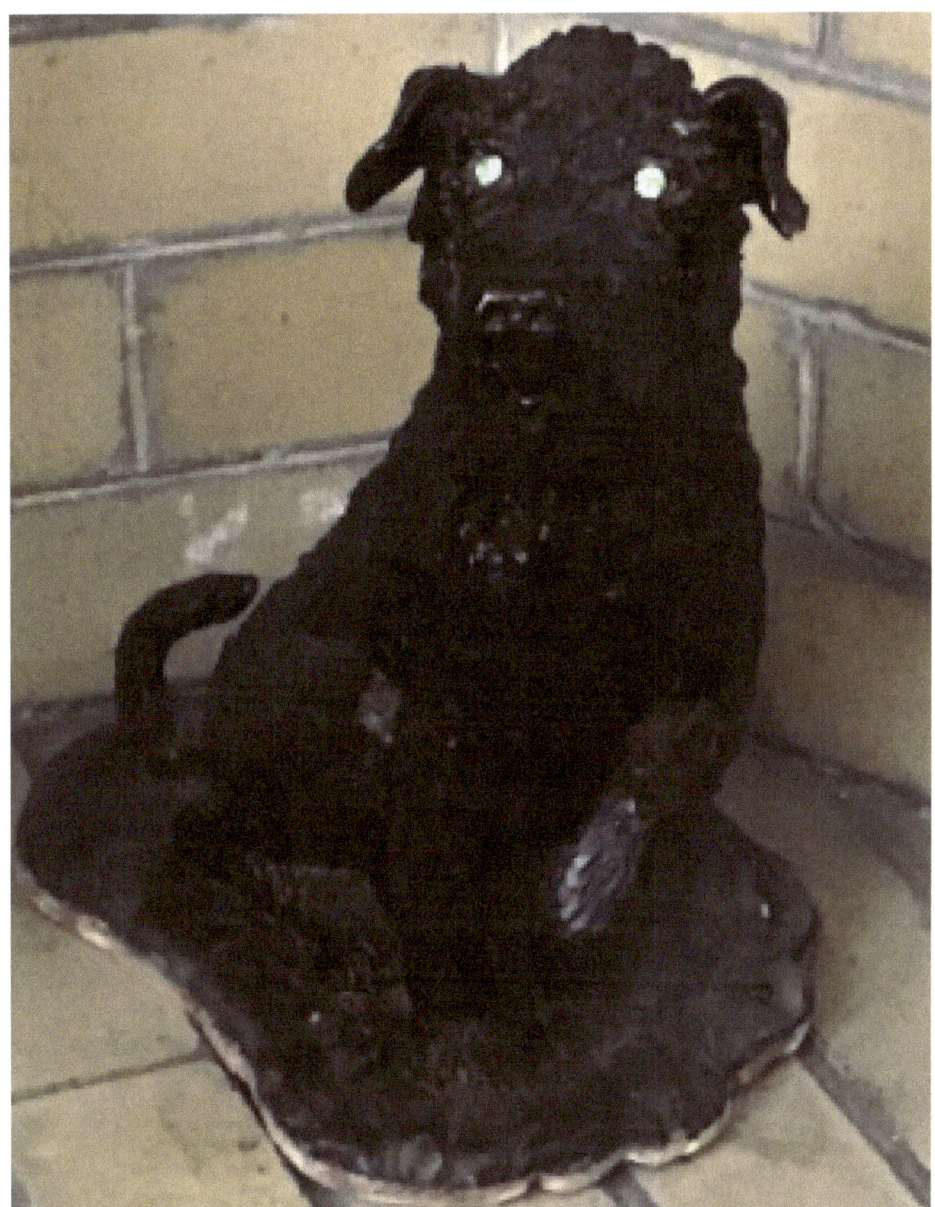

Illustration 17: CHUMLY

Illustration 18: TURTLE

Illustration 19: BOOKENDS

Illustration 20: BOWL SET

Illustration 21: DESK POTTERY

Illustration 22: KITCHEN POTTERY

Illustration 23: TEA CUP - 1989

Illustration 24: POURING CUP

Illustration 25: SUGAR BOWL

Illustration 26: CORN DISH

Illustration 27: SALAD BOWL

Illustration 28: SERVING BOWL

Illustration 29: CERAMIC POUR

Illustration 30: CERAMIC TEA POT

Illustration 31: ABSTRACT VASE

Illustration 32: ASSORTED CERAMIC CREATIONS

LAMPS

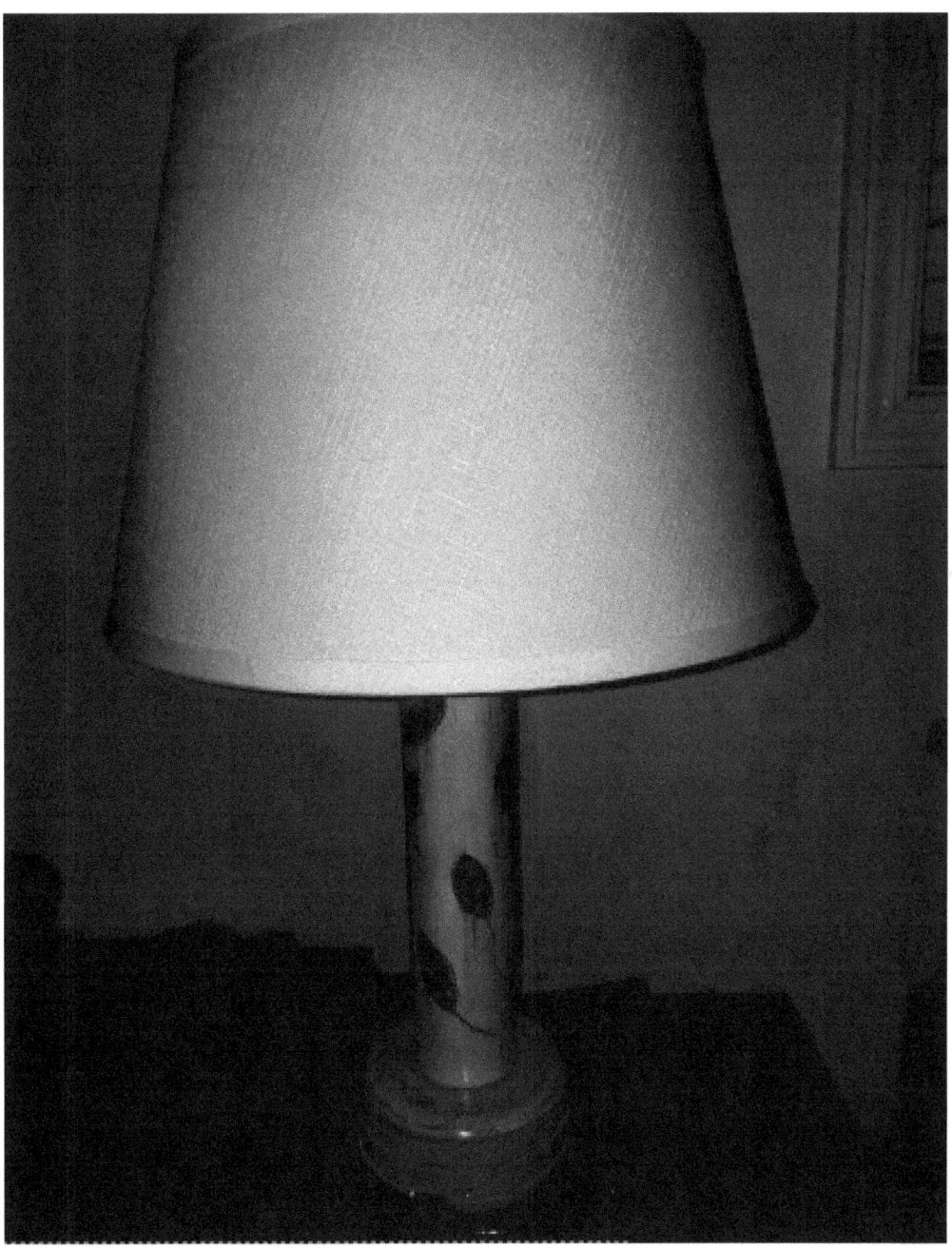

Illustration 33: LAMP MADE BY IG PAINTED BY EMILIA

Illustration 34: CERAMIC LAMP

Illustration 35: ASSORTED LAMPS

PAINTINGS

Illustration 36: THE ALMADA FAMILY CREST

Illustration 37: ABSTRACT 1

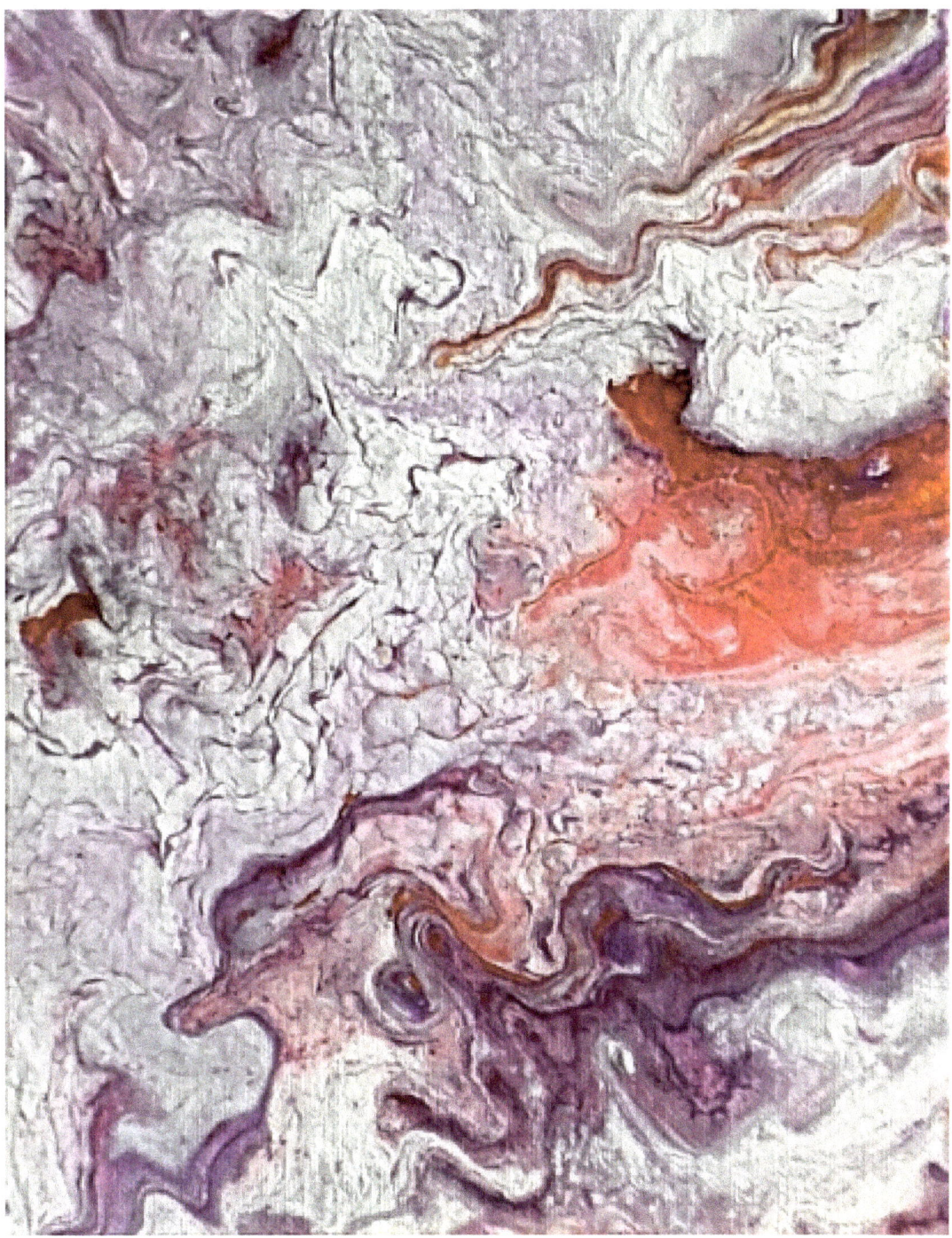
Illustration 38: ABSTRACT 2

Illustration 39: REPRODUCTION OF RENOIR YOUNG GIRL COMBING HAIR

Illustration 40: WATERCOLOR

Illustration 41: CATERPILLAR to BUTTERFLY

Illustration 42: RED ROSES APPLE VASE

Illustration 43: PARROT

Illustration 44: TREE IN FALL

Illustration 45: LOVE FRAME

CHALK

Illustration 46: SPIRALING IN GEOMETRY

NEEDLE WORK

Illustration 47: CROCHET - Given to Robert Almada

Illustration 48: CROCHET - Given to Sally Cruger

Illustration 49: FIVE DOILIES

Illustration 50: UNFINISHED QUILT

Illustration 51: QUILT

Illustration 52: TABLE RUNNER

ACKNOWLEDGEMENTS

I would like to thank my brother Stephen Almada for his encouragement in taking on this project and for providing the stories contained in this book. Without his help this book would not have happened. I would also like to thank my sister Gloria for providing pictures of several of the ceramic creations and paintings featured in this book. Thanks to Sally Cruger for sharing a picture of the crochet that Emilia gave to her many years ago. Thanks to Nancy Oskin for sharing her editing skills and her artistic eye. Thanks to Richard, Stephen, Derek and Gloria Almada for being a source of support and encouragement. Lastly, thanks to Emilia Almada for sharing her stories and art. She is a source of inspiration to us all.

The Editor of this book,

Robert I Almada

Illustration 53: ART BY EMILIA ALMADA

Illustration 54: BIRTHDAY CARD

THE END

Illustration 55: ASSOCIATES DEGREE - TRITON JC

www.ingramcontent.com/pod-product-compliance
Lightning Source LLC
LaVergne TN
LVHW070215080526
838202LV00067B/6826